Nurturi

Readi

Dangling

I may have cancer,
but cancer doesn't have me!

Amy Carr

WESTBOW
PRESS®
A DIVISION OF THOMAS NELSON
& ZONDERVAN

WestBow Press books may be ordered through booksellers or by contacting:

WestBow Press
A Division of Thomas Nelson & Zondervan
1663 Liberty Drive
Bloomington, IN 47403
www.westbowpress.com
1 (866) 928-1240

ISBN: 978-1-5127-2874-3 (sc)
ISBN: 978-1-5127-2875-0 (hc)
ISBN: 978-1-5127-2873-6 (e)

Library of Congress Control Number: 2016901353

Print information available on the last page.

WestBow Press rev. date: 03/07/2016

Contents

Dedicated to

Linda Collins

Distance can never break the ties that bind our hearts. From the first journal you had made for me titled *Dangling* to the completion of this book, you've been by my side through it all, and I am forever grateful for you.

Foreword

By David Carr

How do I introduce you to the concept of *dangling* when it is not something that you can touch, taste, or explain with a few brief sentences? My introduction to *dangling* came from my wife, Amy, in March 2011. After meeting with her doctor and having an ultrasound, she expected a diagnosis of breast cancer within the next week or so. Amy shared with me the Scriptures she had been meditating on those first few days following her initial appointment with her doctor. You see, she was looking and pursuing—no, it was more than that. She was on a mission and desperately searching for answers and peace with everything within her. Those first few days brought us to a specific mental and spiritual focus. Relying on our faith, believing in and applying Scriptures to our fears and worries, and praying helped us secure our footing. By doing this, we transitioned from walking in what felt like quicksand to walking on solid ground. For her, in the midst of all this turmoil, she discovered a place of safety and rest that she had not experienced before. She calls this place of refuge, this act of surrender, "dangling".

Amy had always included me in difficult decisions and situations, and she had leaned on me for more than twenty years as her husband, best friend, spiritual partner, and advisor. She always looked to me for confirmation even if she had come to an answer on her own. We always worked as a team, since we both believed that God had brought us together. We thought that as long as we committed our way to Him, He would lead us together as a couple. It was different this time. I watched Amy as she sought answers and peace from her time praying, reading the Word, and fellowshipping with God. She had questions I knew in my heart I could not answer, but it didn't matter. She had skipped me and tapped directly into the source of her strength. Man, am I glad she did, because it allowed me to see this great work of faith, belief, and personal growth take place in my beautiful wife right before my eyes.

It is kind of cliché to say this great work that took place in my wife was like watching a caterpillar turn into a butterfly. In her case it was more like watching a newborn colt's first attempt to stand—unsure, wobbly, weak, and uncontrolled. (She had walked in faith many times, but doing so in the face of a cancer diagnosis was, well, different from anything she had ever faced.) The colt struggles to stand up only to collapse, exhausted. Then one day before you know it, it is up, stronger than before, and it's running with all the power and grace of the beautiful animal God created it to be—an image of freedom and strength just like a wild mustang on the open range. Like so many events in life, we don't realize what has happened until later when we have the chance to look back and see how God brought all the pieces of the puzzle together. Those first days of Amy's cancer journey were unsure and wobbly. There was a lot of getting up and falling down for both of us. We soon saw that what was before us wasn't just a medical condition or a trial that pitted us against a lethal enemy. It was a journey that was going to leave us deeply changed.

The whole process and reality of not having control as well as the overwhelming vulnerability that comes with cancer were really difficult for us at first. Questions in our minds and fear in our hearts could overwhelm us in a split second. We both knew that guarding our hearts and minds was the top priority for us. I felt a great responsibility to protect Amy, and I struggled personally because I couldn't do that. I couldn't fix this, and I couldn't go through the treatment for her. I didn't know how to reconcile feeling helpless, and I couldn't fathom letting her down when she needed me the most. Fortunately, God works in us individually, and even as close as Amy and I are, we both had different journeys and lessons to learn from this challenge. For Amy, she found her strength and power in place of surrender and trust she calls "dangling." Amy had found her peace. She kept digging until she uncovered her own personal bedrock of faith. She was undeterred with the distractions and specifics of this diagnosis and treatment. Cancer was here, but one thing was clear: regardless of the outcome, she had committed and surrendered in her heart to let God use this trial and to work in her life in this unexpected way. She let cancer become a stepping stone for her to speak about His unfailing love, faithfulness, and the amazing gift of salvation He offers to all who call upon His name.

I was blessed to have a front-row seat, but I still can't do justice in giving you a good definition of *dangling*. I watched an amazing journey and demonstration of courage and faith that one doesn't often see in today's era of making excuses and blaming others. I saw my wife not just make a public reference to God and her faith but also live it out with humility and dignity in some of her darkest days of uncertainty and deep struggle. Let her tell you more about how she discovered dangling in these next few chapters. You'll discover a real person who faced her greatest trial and received one of her greatest gifts in the process. I couldn't be more proud of Amy as a sister in Christ, and I couldn't be more honored to call her my friend and my wife. Her insights and wisdom in this book apply to all of us. Some are funny. Some are challenging. All are genuine and hard-earned.

Acknowledgments

Mine was a journey that I could never imagine facing alone, and I'm so thankful that I didn't have to. First of all, I must thank my husband, David. Thank you for your sacrificial love and commitment to our family, to us, and to me. Thank you for being willing to "charge hell with a squirt gun" on my behalf. You always had the right thing to say just at the right time—a skill I still envy. You were an endless source of love, unshakable faith, wisdom, strength, and comfort for me and all, while you yourself were also sick.

To my children, Kayla and Anthony, thank you for helping me keep the humor and for continuing to do so well in your final years of high school. My prayer was to see you both graduate, and God granted that! I know He has such wonderful plans for both of you. I'm so very proud to be your mom. Thank you to my parents for your unconditional and constant love and support. I don't know where I'd be without you. I love you both more than words can express. To my brother, Jeff, thank you for checking in on me so faithfully throughout this journey, for your optimism and encouragement, and for telling me that very first night that it was all going to be okay. I believed you! I'm so grateful for you, Sharon, and the boys.

To my aunt Deb, thanks for catching me that first day. You make a great coach, cheerleader, stand-up comic, and doting aunt. Here's to you getting past your five-year mark! I'll be there soon!

To the rest of my family, all my girlfriends, and relentless prayer warriors, (I wish I could list all of you), thank you for carrying us day by day on the wings of your constant love and prayers. I am so thankful I had all of you by my side! To my lifelong best friend, Linda, thank you for blessing me with your many personal gifts, cards, and calls; traveling to Knoxville to sit through chemo with me; and returning to celebrate with me by doing our first Komen Race for the Cure together. I can't imagine life without your friendship!

Thank you to my pastors at Chilhowee Hills Baptist Church for praying over me and supporting us throughout this journey. I love and appreciate each of you. Thank you Chilhowee Hills Celebration Choir for standing by me with your constant love and support. To our minister of worship, David Stewart, never in a million years would I have believed I could share my testimony through song in the middle of chemo. Thank you for writing "Trust" and for the opportunity to debut such an awesome song.

To Steve Loope and Ann Lovell, thank you both for your friendship, for your help as editors, and for support as cosojourners in Christ. I could not have finished this project without you!

And finally, thank you to my doctors, who took such incredible care of me—Dr. Lionel McCollum, Dr. Amanda Squires, Dr. Heath Many, Dr. Daniel Ibach, Dr. Joseph Meyer (and the other staff at Thompson Oncology Group), and Dr. Jay Lucas. You supported me, prayed for me, laughed with me, shared heartbreaking news with me, and most of all, celebrated with me.

I am forever grateful for your commitment to fighting cancer and helping your patients move beyond its grip so that they can live their lives to the fullest.

To all of you, thank you. I love you, and I'm so grateful to still be here to do life with you!

Introduction

The first moment I realized that I had breast cancer is one that I will never forget. The doctors, of course, could not confirm a diagnosis until the biopsies were done. But they knew, and so did I. As a wife and mother, my first thoughts were completely focused on my family and the impact this would have on them. It is also a tough battle for a person like me, who likes being in control, to face the realization that I truly had no control over what was happening to me. The vulnerability was so frightening. Whether it is an illness that has invaded your body, a devastating event that has taken away someone you love, or any event that threatens your very existence, your lack of control over it can be very overwhelming and paralyzing.

So who has control? Who will make your steps steady? Who will help you understand what seems to make no sense at all? Who will rescue you from the perilous danger of literally losing your grip on your own sanity? The only one I know who can truly heal your heart, your body, and your soul is God. He is the Great Physician, Healer, Savior, giver of endless grace, author and perfector of our faith, wonderful Counselor, our Creator, the Prince of Peace, and above all else, our heavenly Father. He loves His children and wants to meet their every need. Consider Matthew 7:9 (HBSB), which says, "Who among you, if your child asks for bread, will give him a stone?" I immediately began asking my heavenly Father for very clear direction, for peace, and for understanding. I knew that the root of my life-threatening condition was physical in nature and that I had no control over it, but the battle to overcome the fear and doubt that came with it would be a spiritual one. It was immediately clear to me that the foundation that would sustain me on the journey through cancer treatment and beyond must be built upon biblical truths, God's promises, and an increased faith. So what promises? Which truths? How does one increase one's faith to travel such an unknown road?

God began to reveal to me one day at a time the truth about facing adversity and life's unexpected hurdles that we must overcome. I began to understand that this journey with God would teach me things I would not have learned otherwise. *He was not showing me how to die. He was about to show me how to truly live!* Over the course of eighteen months of treatment, I learned invaluable lessons about myself, my walk with God, how to reconcile adversity, how to be authentic, and how to find true joy in the midst of struggle. I can honestly now say that I am thankful for the journey. You can be too!

If you are facing a life-threatening illness, this book is for you. If you are living day by day with any type of chronic illness, this book is for you. If you are facing one of the biggest disappointments of your life—perhaps you recently lost someone you love, and you can't see how or where to take your next step or get your next breath—this book is also for you! I am not an acclaimed writer. In fact, this is the first book I've ever written. This is my way of sharing all that I have learned on my journey through cancer treatment so that others facing a similar situation may also learn from my experiences, mistakes, and victories. My prayer is that sharing all that I have experienced, from the darkest days of my life to now living life to the fullest, will bring nourishment to your soul and hope to your heart. The fear of cancer was once overwhelming to me. Satan tried to use this fear to consume me. The reality of my mortality was suddenly burned into the forefront of my mind. But God, in His mercy, showed me how to surrender it all to Him, to truly trust Him, and to rest in the palm of His righteous right hand, where only victory could find me. There I could simply *dangle* my feet in complete freedom while He addressed this issue of cancer in my life. My prayer is that you too, with whatever you are facing, will discover the true freedom, comfort, and peace that results from—you got it—*dangling.*

Part 1

The Journey

**Amy's newest additions to her closet signifying
her support for breast cancer awareness.**

Chapter 1

The Darkest of Days

When we are facing an unexpected, unwanted, fear-provoking illness or situation, our whole world can be rocked to the core. My awareness of the journey I was about to take began on March 24, 2011, when I visited my ob-gyn, Dr. Lionel McCollum. I had just had my full annual physical, which included a clear mammogram on January 16, 2011, but a weird patch of bumpy skin had appeared, so I wanted to have it checked out. I feared that Dr. McCollum would think I was being a worrywart since I had just seen him in January, but since it was different from anything I'd ever had, I decided to go on in anyway.

I sat in the examination room in my lovely paper gown, rehearsing what to say to him about why I was back so soon. I couldn't even see this patch of bumpy skin, but I could feel it. Dr. McCollum entered the room in his usual warm, friendly way. I explained that I just wanted to make sure what I was feeling was nothing to be concerned about. When he saw the bumpy patch of skin, he was immediately concerned.

"How long has this been here?" he asked.

"About four weeks," I replied.

His face said it all. He knew I was in trouble, and now so did I. He told me he would refer me to the specialist to whom he sends all his "tough breast patients."

Tough breast patient? You're talking about me? How did I get this title? My mind was racing, and the tears were coming with no end in sight. *Cancer? Me? I have my annual mammograms like clockwork! How did this happen? Was it missed in January?*

I made it to my car in the lower parking garage, debating what to do next. I anxiously called my aunt Deb, hoping she would be at home. She lived close to Dr. McCollum's office. She was on her way home from a school in Maryville, Tennessee, where she has worked as a special education teacher for more than thirty years. She is also a breast cancer survivor. Her mother, my grandmother, whom we all affectionately called Granny, was also a breast cancer survivor. We agreed to meet at her house, which was only about ten minutes away. When I arrived at Deb's, I was crying, trembling, and trying to explain to her what Dr. McCollum had said.

"Am I as strong as you and Granny?" I asked her.

She immediately declared, "Yes, you certainly are! This is just a bump in the road."

Deb had been down this road, and she knew what I would be facing should this turn out to be cancer and if treatment was needed. I felt so overwhelmed and fearful, and though I was not convinced I was strong enough to face such a journey, I think Deb knew the strength would come. I had spoken briefly by phone with my husband, David, who insisted on coming to pick me up from Deb's house. I asked him to just give me some time with her first. After an hour of talking, crying, and talking some more, I felt like I could drive home. Deb followed me on the thirty-minute drive to my house. She was the first safety net I had, and she would no doubt be by my side for whatever came next. I was about to begin a journey with which she was very familiar, and I knew she would help me maneuver through it.

When I arrived home and saw my husband, the tears began to flow again. I was so scared. Words aren't often needed for David and me to know what is in each other's heart and mind. My mind was racing. I'm sure his had been too, but he was not afraid. He knew there was still much more information to obtain, and his main focus was to comfort me.

Could this be an infection? Sure, it could be. Infections often mimicked cancer. Did I think it was an infection? No. I prayed that it would be, but something deep within me knew my life was changing, and that I had no control over it. I needed to decide what my anchor in this unexpected and unwelcomed storm was going to be.

During the next week, David and I worked diligently to keep life as normal as possible for our children. Kayla was finishing up her junior year in high school, and Anthony was a sophomore. We did not want to alarm them. We decided to get through the next few steps before talking with them or our parents. I couldn't even visualize talking to them without falling apart, so I needed some time and more definite information.

My head was spinning as I sat with Deb at my son's indoor drum-line competition on Saturday, trying to appear as if nothing was wrong. Dad and Kayla were with us, but they knew nothing at this point. I fought tears the entire time. I realized how blessed

I was to be there with them to see Anthony perform again and how proud I was of him. The sudden awareness of your mortality also brings with it the overwhelming awareness of the little— and sometimes big—things in life you take for granted. I never wanted to do that again.

I held myself together, but inside I was screaming, "Wake up, people! Stop taking your life for granted! You may never have a moment like this again!"

I couldn't eat or sleep. I lost twelve pounds in five days after seeing Dr. McCollum. The spiritual warfare was totally consuming. I felt as though I was walking in quicksand. I have searched the Bible many times for many different reasons, but now I was in uncharted territory. I spent hours reading through and writing down Scriptures that addressed fear, doubt, faith, help, and healing. (See appendix A.) *I knew I could not control this cancer, but I was not about to let it control me.*

I began praying God's promises back to Him. The very first anchor verse the Lord gave me was this: "See, I am sending an angel ahead of you to *guard* you along the way and to bring you to the place I have prepared" (Exodus 23:20). This was a promise God made to the Israelites when they began their journey through the wilderness. I soon realized it was a promise God was making to me as well! I was not going to be alone on this journey. God was sending an angel ahead of me to guard me, and my destination was a place of new beginnings, of healing, and a more powerful way of living,

The second verse God gave me said, "Then shall your light break forth like the dawn, and, your healing will spring up speedily; your righteousness shall go before you; and the glory of the LORD shall be your rear guard" (Isaiah 58:8 ESV). Okay, I had an angel in front of me and the glory of the Lord Himself behind me, both protecting me! This journey was not going to be some small and forgettable event in my life. God had a purpose for it, and I didn't want to miss it.

I didn't want just to survive or reluctantly go through treatment, dragging down everyone around me with a pessimistic outlook. I wanted to be obedient and joyful while using this journey to highlight God's faithfulness in my life. I knew that *obedience* was the key to truly walking in faith. I was reminded of James 5:14, which says, "Is anyone of you sick? He should call the elders of the church to pray over him and anoint him with oil in the name of the Lord. The prayer offered in faith will make the sick person well and the Lord will raise him up."

I immediately called my pastor, Mark McKeehan. This was my first conscious act of walking out my faith in God's Word and the promises held within it. David and I met with all of our pastors at church later that afternoon so that they could anoint me with oil and to pray over me. It was one of the most special moments of my life! After that time of prayer, I walked away knowing that I had aligned myself through obedience with the Scriptures and had done everything I could to ask for healing. The rest was up to God.

My focus was now on how to increase my faith and walk consistently in it regardless of what lay ahead. This brings us back to the *anchor* I mentioned earlier. An anchor does not bob and weave with the changing of the tides. It holds fast, and it's immovable. Likewise, the anchor of my faith in God during this unexpected storm also needed to be unshakeable.

The next day David took me to Parkwest Comprehensive Breast Center, where I met Dr. Amanda Squires. I was escorted to a private room and given a very lush, warm, white robe. I thought to myself, *This is a nice change from the thin paper gowns we usually get!* I had another mammogram, which showed something on my left side. I was told that I had to wait a few minutes before someone escorted me to another room for an ultrasound.

Once settled in the new room, Dr. Squires came in and introduced herself before beginning the ultrasound. As she moved the jelly-covered probe across the left side of my chest and underarm, she explained that there was definitely a mass there, but they would need to do a biopsy to know what type of mass. She said the mass did not appear to extend to the lymph nodes. From my perspective everything at this point seemed to be moving in slow motion.

"Is it treatable?" I managed to ask her.

"Honey, they're all treatable," she responded.

"I meant *curable*," I clarified.

"One step at a time," the doctor said gently.

She said she would arrange for a biopsy the following week. I asked if, based on what she could see, she could tell me what type of treatment I might need. She said that my oncologist and surgeon would talk with me more about that, but she did not think that keeping my breasts would be an option for me.

Dr. Squires then took my hand to help me sit up, but I began to faint. She laid me back down, and the nurses quickly arrived with cold towels, a fan, water, and crackers. It was all just too much for me to process.

I remember hearing Dr. Squires tell her staff that my fainting should serve as a good reminder. What they see every day—what is very common to them—is very new and overwhelming to their patients. She was right! The thought—the reality—that cancer was invading my body was making my entire body tremble.

I asked for someone to please bring my husband back. David and I sat together in the original exam room, processing the new information. After about twenty minutes, the doctor felt it was safe for me to go home.

The following day I returned to Parkwest Hospital for an MRI. Dr. Squires explained that my surgeon would be Dr. Heath Many and that I would meet him the following day at 4:30 p.m. She also informed me that my biopsies were scheduled the following Monday. *Wow*, I thought to myself. *This is all happening so fast!*

After we arrived at Dr. Many's office the next afternoon, he spent some time getting to know me and David before discussing my situation. After about thirty minutes, Dr. Many examined me, and I once again saw that immediate look of concern that was becoming quite familiar to me. For two hours we soaked in every word Dr. Many said as he laid out the complete treatment plan if the biopsies confirmed I, indeed, had cancer. "Chemo, bilateral mastectomy, chemo again, radiation, hormone therapy." As assuring and gentle as Dr. Many was in laying all of this out for me and David, it still just took our breath away. Though a formal diagnosis of cancer had not yet been given, we decided it was time to talk to our parents and our children.

Anthony was a sophomore in high school when his mom was diagnosed with cancer. Here he is gearing up for an indoor drum-line competition.

Kayla was a junior in high school when her mom was diagnosed with cancer. This is a shot of her with David and Amy on Senior Night the following fall.

Chapter 2

Learning to Wait

Thursday night is family night at my parents' house. They always have dinner ready by 6:30 p.m., and all of us slowly meander in from different directions to enjoy a great meal and catch up with one another. David and I arrived late because we had been talking with Dr. Many well past the end of his workday. I still couldn't eat very much, and my mind was reeling from our conversation with Dr. Many. We knew it was time to tell my parents. My biggest concern was how my mom was going to take the news. I knew it would be just as hard for her to hear it as it was for me to say it. I'm very close to both of my parents, and their love and support have always been unconditional and endless.

David and I sat at the dinner table and slowly began one of the toughest conversations we've ever had to have. We explained to my parents, brother, and sister-in-law what had occurred since my return appointment with Dr. McCollum the previous week—the repeat mammogram, the ultrasound, the MRI, and the meeting with Dr. Many. We shared all that Dr. Many had told us regarding what my treatment plan would include should his suspicion of cancer be correct. We explained that biopsies were next and scheduled for the following week. The heaviness of the moment was dispelled by the assurance from my family that we would face whatever lay ahead together and that all was going to be okay. We had a similar conversation with David's parents, so our focus now turned to telling our children. Anthony, who was about to turn sixteen, had traveled to South Carolina for the Southeast Regional Indoor Drum Line Competition, and he wasn't due back until 2:00 a.m. Sunday morning. This meant we had another two days of waiting, but we knew we needed to talk to the kids together.

After he arrived back at the high school in the wee hours of Sunday morning and helped unpack the drum line's gear, Anthony finally pulled into our driveway around 3:15 a.m. He came into my bedroom to tell me about his trip and show me his new medal. The drum line had taken first place in the regional competition! He then disappeared to his bedroom across the hall and hit the hay. David and I sat up in bed, discussing again how we were going to approach telling the kids the next morning. By 4:30 a.m., we too had finally drifted off for some much-needed sleep.

We decided to stay home from church the next morning and talk with the kids after breakfast. I knew this conversation would most likely bring relief to our daughter, Kayla, who had been hovering over me the past three days, asking, "Is something wrong, Mom?"

The conversation went reasonably well. Anthony was a little more reserved and reluctant to ask questions. Kayla, who always made the best of any situation, immediately began trying to encourage me. Both kids appeared to take the news well, and they had the utmost confidence Mom would be fine. After all, she's Mom, right?

I was relieved to have this conversation behind us, and nothing compared to the hugs I got from my kids after we finished talking. Now my entire family was on board, and their love and encouragement brought great comfort to my soul.

After making it through the long weekend, I returned to Parkwest Hospital on Monday for the biopsies. Dr. Squires explained that while bilateral breast cancer was rare, she wanted my permission to biopsy both breasts so she could confirm that the small area detected on my right side was not cancerous. Of course, I agreed. I changed into the hospital gown, and David and I were sitting on a loveseat in a small private waiting room when his cell phone rang. It was Dr. McCollum calling to check on me. He had no idea we were right next door waiting to have the biopsies. It was so comforting to hear him say he loved me and that he was praying daily for me. Most folks do not get to hear that from their doctors, and I did not take it for granted.

After our conversation I leaned back on David, and he put his arms around me. "You got me?" I asked.

"I've got you," he said with even a tighter grip around me. We sat in silence, in hope, in desperation, and in prayer that the biopsies would confirm an easily treatable cancer at an early stage and that the doctors wouldn't find any cancer on the right side at all.

Sigh. Before I knew it, I was back in that MRI machine with all the clanging and banging that one must endure while it runs. The first run took about thirty minutes, and we did it without dye. Dr. Squires then rolled me out to inject dye and back in for another twenty minutes. Afterward, she helped me slowly stand while she held pressure on the spots where the needles had been placed to ensure no unnecessary bleeding. Whew, it was over!

Now it was time to wait ... again. Waiting, whether for positive or negative news, is always challenging. We had waited to have the MRI before talking to our parents. We had waited until Anthony got home to talk with the kids. We had waited until Monday for the biopsies to be done, and now we were waiting two more days for the results of those biopsies.

Wednesday arrived, and I was preparing to leave Carter High School to take Anthony to the oral surgeon to have his wisdom teeth extracted. As he approached the car, my cell phone rang. A quick glance revealed it was a call from Dr. Many's office. I took a deep breath and answered, "Hello, this is Amy."

"Amy, this is Nurse Mary from Dr. Many's office. The biopsies from Monday confirm that you have infiltrating ductal carcinoma on both sides."

Okay, now the unknown is known. Bilateral breast cancer is rare, and I truly did not expect this diagnosis. My "perfectly healthy" right side was not so healthy after all. I didn't want to alarm Anthony, so I provided Mary with mainly one- to two-word answers and saved my questions for later. I thanked Mary for calling and hung up.

I can't wear the cancer patient hat at the moment, I thought. *I must wear my momma hat and take care of my son today.*

This timing was no doubt divine design. Mary assured me that Dr. Many would be calling that evening to talk further about our next steps. Anthony and I continued on to the oral surgeon's office for his outpatient surgery.

I had managed to text David before I left the school parking lot to tell him that the doctor had confirmed cancer on both sides. He was on his way to meet us at the oral surgeon's office. Once we left Anthony for his surgery to begin, David and I stepped outside and made some phone calls to family members who were also waiting to hear the results.

We spent the rest of the afternoon taking care of Anthony, getting him home, and getting his pain medication started. His surgery went well, but his pain increased dramatically before the pharmacy could fill his prescription. I was very much on edge and agitated while watching him in pain. I felt so helpless on so many levels at that moment. David arrived with his pain meds, and Anthony began to rest. And so did I.

I was emotionally drained, but I was thankful that God had timed the news in this way. While I couldn't deny the fact that I was facing a long ordeal fighting bilateral breast cancer, I certainly got to ignore it for a while—at least in my mind anyway—in order to take care of my son. Being a mom—that's what I'm good at! I know how to care for my children when they are sick. Knowing how to be a cancer patient? Not so much!

Dr. Many called around 6:00 p.m. to lay out the rest of my treatment plan. We went to our bedroom and put Dr. Many on speaker phone. I listened in for about fifteen minutes before asking David to go to take the phone and go to our office to finish the conversation with him. I felt nauseous and just wanted to be alone.

They talked for another thirty minutes while David took very detailed notes, which he would share with me the next day when I was better able to handle the information. That night I just wanted to rest while Anthony recovered and focus on taking care of him.

I constantly prayed, "Lord, please let me be a mom just a little while longer. Please let me finish raising them, see them graduate from high school, get married, and have children of their own. Please, Lord, spare my husband and children from having to watch me suffer, and please spare my parents from having to bury their only daughter." My cries of desperation continued, unseen by my family, but clearly God heard me. He knew my every need and was about to teach me life lessons that I would not have otherwise learned. I just had to trust Him.

This is a prayer shawl made for Amy
by her friend, Judy Wilson.

Chapter 3

Learning to Dangle

The next five days crept by as we waited for the PET scan to be done. We all know what PET scans do. They tell us if the cancer is isolated or if it has spread to other organs in the body. Couldn't I just live in ignorance? Ignorance is bliss, right? The fear was overwhelming at times. When will the good news come? Each phone call erased what we thought was good news.

"It hasn't reached your lymph nodes" became "It has reached your lymph nodes on your left side."

"Your right side is perfectly healthy" became "We see a little something we need to check out on your right side."

"We don't think what we see on your right side is cancerous" became "Your biopsies have confirmed bilateral breast cancer."

Ugh! So how was I to trust a PET scan? If it revealed no signs of the cancer spreading, news would surely follow later that it had. This was the pattern of the previous two weeks to which I had become accustomed. How was I going to stay sane? When would the peace and confidence that I was going to be okay come?

infinite wisdom and mercy, God began to show me
visualize myself resting in my trust in Him. It's one
say that you trust the Lord. It's another thing to live it. I
continued to meditate on the Scriptures that focused on having
faith in God and trusting Him. The next anchor verse the Lord
gave me was Isaiah 41:10 (NLT), which says, "Do not be afraid,
for I am with you. Don't be discouraged, for I am your God. I
will strengthen you and help you. I will hold you up with my
victorious right hand."

So if I am being held in His *victorious* right hand, how then
can I fail? *I can't!* This then, is where I'll stay. Wow, what comfort
came with this revelation! Trying to control this cancer or manage
the treatment for it would lead to nothing but failure. Worrying
would lead to failure. Searching the Internet for understanding—
failure. Trusting what other people know or think they know
about cancer—big failure! Look at the verse again. From where
would my encouragement, help, and strength come? These
constant companions would come from God Himself, who was
holding on to me, not from my ability to hold on to Him, and it
would also come from the reality that nothing can separate me
from Him, not even cancer or the fear that arrived with it.

The only sure way I knew to walk in victory was to place
myself freely into the palm of God's hand, where only *victory* can
find me! This would not be a place where I work diligently to hold
on, constantly repositioning myself in hope of controlling what
is happening to me. I will simply allow my Heavenly Father to
hold me. I will lay myself out in total trust and dependence upon
Him, knowing that what is unknown to me is never unknown
to God and that His power in my life far exceeded anything else,

including cancer! God alone knows if and when I wil
from this cancer. I earnestly asked Him to heal me, bı
my plea made me feel like I didn't trust that God heard my ᴄı,
the first time. It also reminded me of a young child begging for
something in a grocery or toy store. I believe, however, there is
enormous power in applying Philippians 4:6 to my life. "Do not
be anxious about anything, but in every situation, by prayer and
petition, with thanksgiving, present your requests to God." Okay,
so I've prayed, given thanks, and made my request for complete
healing known, but what about this unwanted anxiety that was
now trying to overwhelm my soul?

Picture this: A child crawls up into your lap for you to read a
story to him. Instead of relaxing and trusting your hold on him,
the child constantly repositions himself in order to maintain a
tight grip on your arm or neck to keep from falling. He's just
a bundle of nerves the entire time you attempt to read to him!
He is so focused on whether or not you will let him fall that he
cannot focus on the story you are sharing with him! He is fearful,
distracted, and anxious.

Now, is this what typically happens with children when their
parents attempt to hold them and read books to them or tell them
stories at bedtime? Of course not! Nor does it happen with me
and my heavenly Father. *I picture myself sitting in His right hand,
dangling my feet off the side, totally carefree, while listening to what He is
teaching me and trusting Him to never let go of me.* This was my way
of showing God and those around me that I was aware I was *not*
(and am never) in control of the outcome of this journey, but I
was wholeheartedly submitting to and trusting in the One who
is in control.

It soon became clear that while I faced this painful and unpredictable chapter of my life story, a greater faith and deeper sacrifice would be required of me. This was not the time to hang on in fear, trusting my own grip to keep me safe. It was a time for a renewed trust and dependence on God *alone*. A time to allow myself to just be held, loved, and comforted by my heavenly Father. I began to refer to this time with God as *dangling*.

When the stress and emotions of it all became overwhelming, I would tell my husband or children, "I'm going to dangle for a while." They knew that this meant I was going to my quiet place, usually my bedroom, for a time of prayer, surrender, and rest. *Dangling* taught me to take charge of my thought life which allowed me to become refocused and renewed. Here my emotions, questions, doubts, and fear of the unknown could no longer control me or determine how I was going to handle the unpredictable curves of this cancer journey. As I focused my mind on God's presence and Him holding me in His protective, righteous, and victorious right hand, every ounce of tension and anxiety would simply leave my body. Sometimes I would even curl up and cover myself from head to toe with the prayer shawl that a sweet friend from church had knitted for me and breathe in the love with which every stitch was made.

For me, the five-day wait for the PET scan was the longest and most difficult wait of all, but it brought with it the opportunity to perfect my ability to dangle. This one deliberate decision to respond to fear in this way allowed me to experience intimate fellowship with my heavenly Father. It also kept me focused on His love for me, promises to me, and protection of me. Dangling also allowed my nerves to be calmed, and it dispelled any lingering fear or anxiety. As a result, I experienced true rest that served me better than any drug ever could. It is a method of coping with stress that I still depend on today four years later.

I had made my request for complete healing known, and I was now trusting God to protect me while He dealt with this issue of cancer in my life. My confidence was now soaring because it did not stem from what *I* was going to do but from what *God* was going to do during this season of my life. Whatever He chose was going to change me for the better, and it would have eternal value too. I would act on what He assured me to be true, not what I feared might be true. Instead of choosing worry, I chose worship. I traded in life-robbing doubt for genuine hope and cashed in all my fear for life-sustaining faith. Instead of trying to control my situation, I chose to pursue the freedom that resulted from—you got it—*dangling*! Philippians 4:7 began to manifest itself in my life right away. "And the peace of God, which transcends all understanding, will guard your heart and your mind in Christ Jesus." So the peace I needed was not going to be found in my efforts to manage the next year of my life. In fact, I would soon find the opposite to be true.

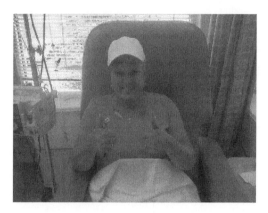

Amy getting her chemo at Thompson
Cancer Survival Center.

Amy with some of Thompson Oncology staff. They
truly became friends after a very short time.

Chapter 4

Relinquishing Control

Monday finally came, and David drove me to Thompson Cancer Survival Center for the PET scan. I'll never forget the nurse who started the IV to inject the dye for the scan. I may never see him again, but I will remember our conversation forever. I knew right away he was a Christian and had been placed in my path to get me through the next couple of hours. We talked about heaven and about how our infinite minds couldn't truly grasp the reality of eternity with God.

An hour after the dye was injected into my arm, I was taken into another room where I would undergo the PET scan. I was told that the machine took nine hundred pictures in eleven minutes. The covers of the three florescent lights above me were made to create a beautiful beach scene, most likely in an effort to comfort and calm the patient going into the machine. Though it was pleasing to the eye, the only thing that brought me comfort was the assurance that God already knew what the doctors were about to learn. He had a plan. I just wanted to know more about His plan!

Once the scan was over, I was back in the car with David, and we were headed home. I'll never forget—not that David would let me forget anyway—a recording of Dr. Adrian Rogers on the radio that seemed to be meant just for me. I had not listened to Dr. Rogers in years, but here he was on some random AM radio station that we rarely listen to, talking about how most people misquote James 4:7 (HCSB). "People say, 'Resist the devil, and he will flee from you,'" Dr. Rogers said, noting that they often overlook the first part of the verse, which says, "Therefore, submit to God."

You simply cannot hold on to control and submit at the same time! To submit is to place oneself humbly under another's authority. This was yet another reminder not to waste any of my much-needed focus and energy on trying to control this cancer or any part of the treatment I was about to experience.

Dr. Rogers reminded us that day that the Devil cannot prophesy your life. Only God knows your future. So it stood to reason in my little pea brain that if Satan couldn't prophesy my life, then he couldn't prophesy my death either. He was hurling all the arrows of fear and doubt he could at me, but I soon realized that he had nothing else to throw at me. As I submitted to God and resisted the fear and doubt, Satan would flee. Satan is not like God. He is neither omnipresent nor omnipotent. He is limited, and the more I began to ignore his threats instead of trying to battle with him, the more liberated I became.

To battle Satan on our own terms is not what God has instructed us to do. He first instructs us to "submit" or relinquish control to God, who has already defeated evil, and then to "resist the devil" by standing firm on the promises of God. Finally, "the devil will flee from you." This sent me hurling back to *dangling*. I was determined not to waste another ounce of energy on the Great Deceiver, for I knew he had no power over me and no place in my life. *The Devil cannot prophesy my life or my death, so I will not live as if he can!*

The next day we went to Thompson Cancer Survival Center to meet my new oncologist, Dr. Daniel Ibach, who would share with us the results of the PET scan. David and my dad both went with me. Once we were taken to an examination room, I sat down between David and my dad, and we waited quietly for Dr. Ibach. I could feel my anxiety slightly rising, but I was truly ready to move forward with whatever came next.

After a few minutes, Dr. Ibach entered the room and announced, "Your PET scan shows no signs of metastatic disease!" Okay, that sounded good, but what did it really mean? I smiled since I knew this was good news, but then I asked, "So what does this exactly mean?"

Dr. Ibach replied that cancer cells only appeared or "lit up" in both breasts and some adjacent lymph nodes under my left arm, which was considered to be part of the breast region. Whew! Okay, so there was no sign of any cancer anywhere else in my body! We all three gave an audible sigh of relief!

While I indeed felt relieved, a small part of me still wondered if I'd later receive another phone call bringing bad news since this had been the trend. Dr. Ibach talked with us for almost an hour, explaining what infiltrating ductal carcinoma is and how it spreads. He explained that I was ER and PR positive, meaning that both estrogen and progesterone served as the fuel for the cancer. Given that the cancer had made it to some lymph nodes on my left side, it was vital that we start chemo as soon as possible in order to protect the rest of my body.

I wouldn't let Dr. Ibach discuss staging with me on this day, but I learned later that the cancer was stage three on my left side and stage two on my right. Dr. Ibach explained that this was an aggressive but common type of cancer and that his plan included prescribing a stronger chemo than they had first planned. He told me to return to the hospital the next day for baseline blood work and an EKG since the chemo could be hard on my heart.

The technician who conducted my EKG the next day was also a breast cancer survivor. As she shared her story with me, I knew once again the angel God had sent ahead of me to guard me was at work. Her story gave me hope and spurred me on to have confidence in my ability to face whatever came next.

Dr. Ibach's office then scheduled me for a surgically implanted "power port" the following day, and chemo started the morning after that. I thought to myself, *Wow! So much, so fast! They are worried about me! My prognosis may be hopeful, but there is a reason they are moving me along this fast.* Here came fear creeping through the back door again. I had to choose to be thankful for the quick response and cooperation among the medical team, whose members were responsible for my care, and I had to resist the urge to worry about anything. My medicine was finally coming!

This marked the end of the initial three weeks of my journey. To me, the beginning of chemo was the beginning of cancer meeting its match! Never did I call chemo "poison" as many do. This was my medicine! Nor did I claim the cancer by saying, "*My* cancer is this type," or, "They're treating *my* cancer this way." This intruder was not welcome in my body, and I wanted no ownership of it. *I wanted it gone!* Chemo-surgery-chemo-radiation-hormone treatment—this is the avenue through which God was choosing to heal me, and I had no desire to question it. I was ready just to get the show on the road!

Amy on her way to dinner just after
her husband cut her hair.

Five days after the haircut, Amy's hair was gone.
Kayla and Anthony are kissing her here, but
they would often rub her head for good luck.

Chapter 5

Donning a New Look

My first chemo was on Friday, April 15, 2011, nine days before Easter and my forty-seventh birthday. Everything went smoothly, and I experienced no nausea or fatigue. We all know, however, the main side effect that chemo patients rarely avoid—the loss of hair. I was told to expect my hair to start falling out about two weeks after my first chemo treatment. The following Sunday was Easter, and I was so thankful that my parents and Aunt Deb could attend the Sunday morning worship service with us at our church. They have always been very involved in their own churches, so to attend a service together is always a treat. It was such an awesome morning!

After the service we all gathered at my parents' home for the greatly anticipated Easter lunch. After enjoying a few bites of practically everything on our home-cooked, mouth-watering buffet, I opened a few presents from my family. David and the kids gave me two beautiful scarves. Mom and Dad gave me great selection of colorful bandanas with matching ball caps. My aunt Deb gave me a beautiful box that would hold all the "get well" cards I had begun receiving. My brother and sister-in-law gave me a wall hanging that reminded me, "With God all things are possible. Without God, nothing is possible." My hair was still intact, but not for long. By Wednesday, my scalp was hurting, and my hair began falling out. This was not as emotional for me as I thought it would be. I debated how to respond.

On a whim while the kids were at school, David and I decided to make a video. No one will ever see this video, but I will tell you about it. We went into the downstairs bathroom, where David kept his clippers. After selecting the right setting, he got his phone out to take a before and after picture. He pressed the video button and began asking me questions about the changes happening in my life.

I began explaining that while this invasion of my body was not a welcomed one, I knew God was going to use it in my life to fulfill His purpose and that together we were going to kick some cancer butt! We talked about trials David and I had already faced together, and I said that sometimes when stress overwhelmed me, I just wanted to pull my hair out!

At that point I literally began pulling my hair out while David was recording. It easily came out by the handful! We laughed, hugged, and knew this was an intimate moment that we would reflect back on and smile about for years to come.

David proceeded to set the clippers on the appropriate setting and cut my hair. With all the highlights now gone, my hair was much darker and obviously much shorter. After a hot shower, I took Kayla to UT campus for her flute lesson, and David took Anthony to Rush's music store for his drum lesson. We met afterward at Don Pablo's Mexican restaurant for dinner.

I tried not to touch my hair since doing so meant to dislodge a little more each time. We joked about everyone checking their plates occasionally to make sure Mom's hair hadn't fallen into their food!

We ran into friends who commented that they liked my new look. I knew it was only going to be a few more days before I'd be completely bald, so I thoroughly enjoyed the moment. We went to the mall after dinner and had some fun trying on various wigs.

By the following Sunday, my hair was gone. I had purchased a few more scarves, and I began learning how to tie them around my head. A dear friend, Terry, gave me two summer tops with matching earrings and a scarf that matched both of them. Matching up scarves, bandanas, hats, and so on with my clothes became quite fun right away. I ordered a wig that looked a lot like my former hair, highlights and all. A lot of people never knew it wasn't my real hair, nor did they have any idea that I was going through cancer treatment. I continued to work, go to my kids' events, spend time with friends, attend church, and sing in the choir.

We continued as well to use humor to deal with the change in my appearance. At home the kids would jokingly walk by and rub my bald head for good luck. David walked into the den for movie night one time wearing one of the less attractive wigs I had ordered. It looked bad enough on me but far worse on him! When everyone began to realize that I was truly okay with my new look, they quickly became more at ease and okay with it too.

Summer had arrived, and I enjoyed shopping for new scarves to match various summer outfits. I was determined to attend three weddings while I was going through chemo, and I did. I also sang a song at church that our music minister was inspired to write the day he and the other pastors prayed over me. This would be the first time I sang a solo in a scarf since my diagnosis. The choir members, who so graciously and lovingly walked with me through this journey, altered their appearance to show their support for me. All of the men wore pink shirts or ties, and the women wore scarves on their heads. It was an incredible experience and a lesson learned about being transparent in a society that does not always embrace authenticity. I would also sing in three concerts with the choir while I was going through chemo, each time donning my new look. I would unexpectedly meet all kinds of other cancer survivors, because when you wear a head scarf or bandana with a ball cap, you become a magnet for other survivors who genuinely want to encourage you when they see you. I have heard some amazing stories!

The summer seemed to fly by, and before I knew it, I had completed six rounds of chemo while altering my schedule very little and missing very little work. I often arrived for chemo with homemade salsa and chips in hand for the Thompson Oncology staff that took care of me. I quickly gained respect and admiration for the chemo nurses, and I think they respected and admired me as well. They were playing a role in saving my life physically, but they also encouraged me every time I saw them. In return, they appreciated the laughter and positive attitude I brought to the chemo room and often commended my resolve to "not be robbed" by cancer. I thought about how much the oncology staff invested in their patients and how unsettling it must be to know that some of their patients would not survive despite their best efforts. God had protected me throughout this first leg of

Dangling

my journey, and I was only sick for three to four days the week following each of the last three chemo treatments. It was now September, and it was time to face the reality of a much more significant change in my appearance and my life that loomed just over the horizon.

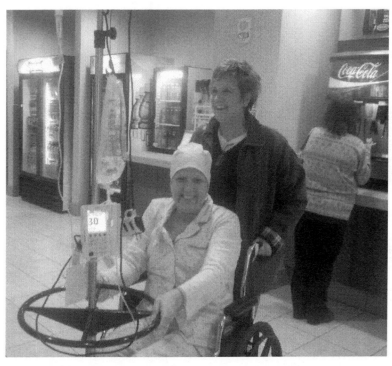

Amy being taken back to her room NASCAR-
style by her Aunt Deb when they had stayed
too long in the hospital cafeteria.

Chapter 6

Good-Bye Girls

On September 23, 2011, I arrived at Parkwest Hospital at 8:00 a.m. I was scheduled for a bilateral mastectomy with immediate reconstruction at 1:00 p.m. My main surgeon, Dr. Heath Many, would begin the surgery, and my plastic surgeon, Dr. Jay Lucas, would complete it. I knew when I awoke from this surgery that the tumor would finally be gone. For me, living with a cancerous tumor in my body was much more traumatic than living without my breasts.

Dr. Many and Dr. Lucas stopped by to see me before I was sedated. They ran into a snag while they were prepping me for surgery. My blood count was low. Since the doctors could not access my port during surgery because it was located within the surgery field, they began IVs in both of my arms. One would be used for a blood transfusion while the other was used for antibiotics, fluids, and pain medicine. I was told if a third line was needed, they might start one in my foot or my neck. I told them that if they were going to put a needle in my neck, they needed to wait until I was asleep and have it out by the time I woke up! The nurse proceeded to inject vancomycin into my right arm.

Unfortunately, she gave it to me a little too fast, which caused me to develop "red man syndrome." I began itching like crazy, and my chest, neck, and face turned red within minutes. To provide some relief, I was given Benadryl, which I knew would quickly put me to sleep, so I immediately began saying good-bye to David and my parents. "See ya on the other side," I said. I slowly faded away into unconsciousness as they rolled me toward the operating room. I was at peace because I knew that what was unknown to me was not unknown to God and that His hold on me would never be loosened for any reason. What was obviously out of my control was fully under His, and I had no doubt that He would be watching over me in that operating room.

When I awoke in recovery, I felt no pain, but I noticed right away the drains lined up across my chest. Before I knew it, I was in a room with David looking down at me. I remember asking him, "Is it gone?"

He replied "Yes, honey, and all went well."

What a weight lifted off of me! I felt no anxiety about dealing with the changes that the future held. I just wanted to savor the moment, the reality that the cancer was now gone. When my daughter, Kayla, came to see me, she noted that the blood-filled drains draped across my chest made me look like a Christmas tree with red bells strung across it. There is nothing quite like my daughter's humor! My family is one that has fun wherever we go, even the hospital! My aunt Deb came to see me while I was in the hospital later for another surgery, and while there, she decided to roll me downstairs to the cafeteria—wheelchair, IV pole, and all. We stayed a little longer than planned, and they called me over the intercom and told me to return to my room, so we did,

NASCAR-style! Having a sense of humor makes life challenges seem less threatening.

I returned home the day after the bilateral mastectomy, still looking like a Christmas tree. My husband waited on me hand and foot despite not feeling well himself. Family and friends brought meals, gift cards, flowers, and "get well" cards. I spent most of the month of October in the recliner, recovering while watching a lot of TV. I came to realize how almost everything on TV during the month of October was devoted to raising breast cancer awareness. I listened to story after story from survivors encouraging viewers to sign up for the Susan G. Komen Race for the Cure and challenging everyone to "get your mammogram today." Given that my mammogram in January gave us no clue that cancer was already attacking my body, this constant plea did not sit too well with me.

This time at home was a time of further reconciling for me. How could I embrace the sisterhood of breast cancer survivors when I never wanted to be part of this pink world? I wanted to scream, "Wake up!" and, "Don't trust mammograms!" While mammograms are extremely beneficial to detecting certain types of breast cancer, I had a clear mammogram just ten weeks before being diagnosed with bilateral breast cancer. I learned later that the type of cancer I had could not be detected by a mammogram until it had progressed a little further. *Sigh.* I don't know how to describe my feelings the moment I realized that I had trusted in a false sense of security.

Most of all, I truly just wanted to feel *normal* again. Even though I would later embrace and be grateful for this sisterhood, being part of this pink world did not yet feel normal or even acceptable to me at this point in my journey. This view, like many others, changed for the better as time passed.

**David and Amy enjoying a little break
at the beach after Amy's consultation at
Mayo Clinic in Jacksonville, Florida.**

Chapter 7

A Setback or a Setup
for a Comeback?

Two weeks after having the bilateral mastectomy, I returned to Dr. Ibach for a follow-up appointment. This was one of the toughest days of my entire journey. I had already been told that my post-chemo MRI showed "no sign of residual malignancy found." However, Dr. Ibach explained to us that MRIs didn't show everything. The reality was that when Dr. Many removed my breasts and adjacent lymph nodes, about one-third of the tumor was still there, and I had seven lymph nodes on the left side that still tested positive for cancer, even after six months of receiving a very strong chemo. So while I had been enjoying a period of relief and celebration, in reality, this cancer was still after me! I felt like someone had kicked me in the stomach.

Dr. Ibach explained that he wanted me to go to Mayo Clinic for a second opinion regarding whether or not I should go through another round of chemotherapy. The fact that he felt I should take the second round was enough for me, but he wanted us to visit

Mayo to see what one of their lead oncologists had to say about a second round. I was devastated. The nurse from the Mayo Clinic called me before we even got out of the parking lot to set the appointment. She said, "I see here you have metastatic breast disease?" I almost lost consciousness! *Metastatic*? Why did she use that word? I only had cancer in a few adjacent lymph nodes, which were now gone. How dare she say that to me! I felt paralyzed. David drove me across the street to see my surgeon so he could check my bandaging. Dr. Many was very supportive but also less celebratory than I expected. I was still so shaken by the phone conversation with the Mayo nurse that he suggested we go back across the street and speak with Dr. Ibach again, so we did.

I remember feeling so cold, my body trembling, and not being able to think very clearly. Dr. Ibach explained that "metastatic breast disease" didn't mean the cancer has metastasized anywhere other than the adjacent lymph nodes on my left side. He used the phrase to describe my condition because even though the cancer was still in the breast region, which includes some lymph nodes, it had indeed traveled to those lymph nodes and set up camp. Using this diagnosis was also helpful in expediting the process of me being evaluated at Mayo Clinic. All I could hear in my head was what Dr. Ibach said the day I first met him, "I know you all are on pins and needles, so I just want you to know that the PET scan shows no sign of metastatic disease." Wow, how the relief we felt at that moment contrasted greatly with the fear and confusion I was now experiencing as we talked about the need for second round of chemo. I had known from the beginning that there would most likely be two six-month rounds of chemo, but based on the results of the post-chemo MRI, which had revealed no signs of residual malignancy, I had wrongly assumed I wouldn't need the second round of chemo. I was shattered.

David knew how I was feeling, and as always, he found the perfect way to comfort me. When we left the room where we had now talked with Dr. Ibach twice in one day, he pointed out a painting to me just outside the door—an elderly couple sitting on the front porch of a beautiful Victorian house. David put his arm around me and said, "See these folks sitting in the porch swing, looking out over the beautiful landscape, probably reflecting on their years together?" I nodded. He said, "That's us thirty years from now." He then declared, "God is not finished with us yet, Amy." *Sigh.* I don't know where I'd be without this man by my side.

The appointment with one of the lead oncologists at Mayo Clinic was set for October 24. We arranged for the kids to stay with friends, kenneled the dogs, and hit the road south to Jacksonville. This route was familiar to us since we had already visited Mayo in 2005 after eight months of doctors struggling to find the cause of David's sudden, severe, chest pain that had begun in September 2004. David has lived with severe, chronic chest pain for over eleven years now. He then broke his wrist and greatly damaged his left leg in a ladder fall in 2010. As a result, part of his lower left leg was removed, leaving him with vascular damage that affected both legs. Now here we were at Mayo again, the sick taking care of the sick, but David would have it no other way. We were extremely fortunate to have lodging arrangements at Gabriel's House at Mayo Clinic. It is an absolutely beautiful facility built by the Bacardi family (yes, the rum people), created from a need for long-term housing for the families of patients being evaluated or treated for cancer at Mayo Clinic. Everything is sterilized. The rooms are oversized with beautiful hardwood flooring, and the facility includes a large state-of-the-art kitchen with four cooking stations, a large living room with a flat screen TV and fireplace, a game room, a computer room, a library, a dining room, and a large deck with rocking chairs. It was breathtakingly gorgeous! I would definitely not be the only one here with a scarf on my head. That was also nice. Most of the staff at Gabriel's House are cancer survivors themselves, so they had special insight into how to meet the needs of their guests.

We met with the Mayo oncologist the next day. He gave us important advice. He explained that for many years he recommended a second round of chemotherapy for patients like me but also said that he no longer did as frequently. He explained that it is uncommon to eradicate all of the cancer cells with one series of chemo, so surgery, radiation treatments, and hormone therapy were usually prescribed as well. He stressed the importance of these medical interventions along with taking high doses of Vitamin D and maintaining a healthy diet. He also explained that the hormone therapy phase of treatment is like getting "a little dose of chemo every day for the next five to ten years." Since I had done so well with the first six months of chemo, he said that I should by all means take the second round if I wanted. He reminded me, though, that should the cancer recur, many medical treatments were available that could extend my life for many years. I thought to myself, *Well, okay, I'm glad you feel good about that.* However, I wanted to walk away knowing I had done absolutely everything I could to prevent this from ever happening to me again! So this doctor didn't seem quite as concerned about my status. Maybe this was good, or perhaps he had seen so many conditions worse than mine that he had a better perspective than I did. Regardless, David and I agreed that I would do the second six-month round of chemo.

After the consultation at Mayo, David and I wanted to use some of this time away for the two of us. We needed the rest and time to allow this new information to sink in, so we decided to enjoy a leisurely day at the beach before heading back up to Tennessee. We then stopped in Savannah, Georgia, for a few hours to take in the beautiful scenery, artwork, and architecture, and we even savored a few bites of homemade fudge. We then continued north along the coast to Beaufort, South Carolina, where we had dinner with dear friends, John and Lucille Payne, before bedding down for the night. (There's just no other Southern belle quite like Lucille, unless it's her mother.) Time spent talking and laughing with good friends was good medicine!

As we began the last leg of our trip home the next morning, we noticed that the fluid accumulating in my one remaining drain was changing colors. I called Dr. Lucas from my cell phone and made an appointment for the next day. When Dr. Lucas saw me, he was very concerned. He began draining yellowish fluid out of the left side of my chest with a needle. He wasn't sure if I had an infection because the drain had been in so long or if something else was going on. He removed the drain in case it was the cause of the infection. Over the next several weeks, I found myself back in his office multiple times, having fluid drained from the left side of my chest. On about my fourth visit, Dr. Lucas decided to redo my left side. This meant another surgery to put in a new expander then loading me up with antibiotics. It also meant the introduction of Dr. Adams, an infectious disease doctor, to my team of physicians.

After five days in the hospital, I was released with a regimen of antibiotics through my port three times a day. I continued working, and I was able to administer the antibiotics myself. Each dose took about twenty minutes, so I would often do one in the morning before starting work and again eight hours later while driving from one appointment to another. Then if I fell asleep before the final dose, my husband would always hook me up one last time, flush my port, and tuck me in for the night. We made a pretty good team!

Dr. Ibach also later wanted me to take Femara, an aromatase inhibitor, which would keep my adrenal glands from producing estrogen, which is what fueled the type of cancer I had. There was one catch. It was only to be taken by postmenopausal women. So two weeks later Dr. McCollum removed my remaining ovary. Now I would be hurled into menopause, hot flashes and all, but I would be a candidate for this new hormone therapy when the time came.

Meanwhile, Christmas was approaching, and the right side of my chest was now turning red and showing signs of infection despite the strong antibiotics I was injecting through my port several times a day. I thought to myself, *What is going on? Something is very wrong here.* I had no appetite, so I began losing weight from not eating. My chest hurt so badly that I could hardly sit up or stand without excruciating pain. David did much of our Christmas shopping online while I moved as little as possible. New blood work revealed that I needed a transfusion, so my mom drove me to Parkwest Medical Center again for the two-hour process. The weeks before and after Christmas, Dr. Lucas continued to drain fluid from my chest. The pain worsened, and the right side of my chest was still very red. He recommended he redo the expander on the right side in the same manner he had done the left side.

As soon as Dr. Lucas returned from visiting his family for the Christmas holidays, I went to his office to discuss what would be my fourth surgery. By that time the left side of my chest was once again turning red, and the pain was worsening. I made the decision to have everything taken out. I declared to myself, "This is crazy. I'm going to die from an infection when I'm being healed of cancer! Take it all out!"

On December 28, 2011, I underwent my final surgery, not to redo anything but to remove the expanders completely. Efforts toward my "immediate reconstruction" were now abandoned, and we were all praying that the source of this infection would be revealed. I rested over New Year's with a deep sense within me that I had made the right decision. Within the next few days, the wall of fire extending from one shoulder to the other began to subside, and I knew I was going to be okay.

On January 6, Dr. Lucas called to inform me that my culture had finally revealed something. Apparently, the expanders in my chest made me the perfect incubator for an acid-fast bacilli type of infection. "This is very rare," he said, "but there is treatment for it." He told me to stop injecting the antibiotics through my port immediately because this was not the appropriate treatment for the type of infection I had. This explained why I had continued to get worse, not better! The treatment for this infection came in pill form— actually six pills a day for six months. Meanwhile, Dr. Ibach was ready for me to start my second round of chemo. It too was in pill form—eight pills a day for the same six months. So beginning in January 2012, I took eighteen pills a day. Six were the antibiotic, eight were chemo, and the other four were vitamins/supplements. This would be my regimen for the next six months. I was on my way back and more determined than ever to regain my health.

Amy with her mom and daughter at the ninety-eighth birthday party for her grandmother. Her grandmother passed away later that same year.

Chapter 8

Time to Celebrate

With the beginning of a new year came a new lifestyle, new hope, and new hair! No more wigs, no more scarves, no more bandanas, and no more hats. I honestly rather missed the fun of matching up outfits and jewelry with scarves and hats. My hair came in incredibly curly, and it was getting thicker every day. I had adjusted to my new routine of taking a mountain of pills every morning and evening, and I was enjoying working, helping my kids with band and school, singing with my church choir, exercising, and just having energy again! We celebrated my grandmother's ninety-eighth birthday in February. It was such a wonderful day getting to spend time with her, my parents, aunts, uncles, and cousins, just celebrating family. My entire family had been very supportive of me since the beginning of this cancer journey.

During spring break my daughter decided to forego her senior band trip to Atlanta for a trip to the hospital to have her tonsils taken out. The surgery was followed by a very painful recovery. While I enjoyed the time off from work that week to rest and take care of her, my heart ached for her when her pain set in. She did, however, completely recover, and all was forgotten by early April. At school one day, we surprised Kayla with her graduation gift. David had found a great deal on a preowned Ford Escape and bought it for her. Kayla was called to the school office and given a parking permit and was told to locate that particular parking spot in case she ever needed to use it. Kayla was of course very confused given she didn't own a car. When she reached the parking lot, she was shocked to find the Escape sitting in her newly assigned parking spot. The look on her face was priceless. She enjoyed her independence of driving to school and work. Unfortunately a few weeks later, we received one of those phone calls that make every parent's heart stop! Kayla was involved in an accident coming home from school. Her SUV was totaled. Thankfully her injuries were minimal, but her days of driving to school and work were cut short.

Graduation time was now upon us. Kayla was focused on setting up her classes for her first year in college, while Anthony was wrapping up his third year in indoor drum line and preparing to be a senior in high school. With all of this going on, my second six-month round of chemo and six months of antibiotics absolutely flew by, causing little disruption in my daily routine of juggling all that comes with working full-time while being a wife and a mom. I did become quite sick toward the end of the first twelve weeks on the new chemo, so Dr. Ibach gave me a two-week break before we started the final twelve weeks. This timely break worked out perfectly because it allowed me to feel my best when singing with the choir at our Easter service. I also wanted to be able to eat what I knew would be an incredible lunch afterward!

By June 2012, I had taken more than 2,800 pills, and I was ready to celebrate being finished with chemo and the antibiotics! I took some sick leave from work to recover from the chemo and some vacation time to celebrate with my family this milestone in my treatment. We also wanted to celebrate Kayla's graduation from high school, so we took the kids and two of their friends to Orlando for a week at Universal Studios and Sea World. It was hot, muggy, and tiring, but I was so grateful that David and I both felt well enough to go. This trip was made possible by Memories of Love, a nonprofit agency that was established to bless cancer patients by covering the hotel costs and park tickets for them to create new memories with their families. We just had to find the time, cover the cost of gas and food, and feel well enough to go! It was such a great time of fun, celebration, and focusing on something other than—you got it—cancer!

When we returned home, I immediately began the next leg of my journey through thirty-five radiation treatments. This meant going to Thompson Cancer Survival Center in downtown Knoxville Monday through Friday. I scheduled my appointments for 4:40 p.m. so that I could be their last patient for the day. This gave me plenty of time to take care of daily work responsibilities, but the treatment was early enough so that I could stop by the facility on the way to any evening appointments I may have scheduled. Most of the time, I was in and out of the scanner and back to my car in less than thirty minutes. As the treatments progressed, my skin slowly began to turn red. Then it turned dark red and then purplish. Then it started to blacken, and soon after that, peeling began. Toward the end of radiation, I really struggled on a few days to go back, but I knew I had to.

I proudly walked into Thompson Cancer Center for my final treatment on September 11, 2012. I was greeted by one of the nurses, and she presented me with a brightly colored certificate of completion that had been signed by all the staff in the radiation oncology department. A day that had brought so much trauma and sadness to our country now represented a time of triumph for me personally. I knew I'd never forget my final day of treatment. I was so burned that I could barely tolerate the lightest of shirts, and I could not wear my prosthetics at all. But joy filled my heart, and the tears flowed freely because I was so inexpressibly grateful to be finished. No more chemo, no more blisters in my mouth, no more throwing up, no more surgeries, no more drains, no more blood transfusions, no more infection, no more antibiotics, no more radiation, no more holding the seat belt away from my chest because of the burns, no more driving home totally exhausted—the time had come to celebrate!

Team Amy from the Komen Race for the Cure.

Amy and her husband, David, who
brought her roses after the race.

Chapter 9

Cancer Comes in Many Colors

Fall is my favorite season, but with it came October and another month of breast cancer awareness events. The memories of my recovery from surgery the previous October while watching all of the "pink" media that implored women to understand the importance of early detection flooded my mind. I had felt quite resentful at that time about being hurled into this pink world of which I had not asked to be a part. However, now a year later, the more I learned about this world, the more I embraced it.

I was blessed to meet so many other breast cancer survivors, and I had benefitted from their stories of hope, accomplishment, and encouragement. I learned more about the research and the advances that scientists had made in chemotherapy to lessen the negative side effects it had on patients. I had come to know some of the physicians, nurses, lab technicians, and others who had chosen to work in this field to help save the lives of those affected by cancer. I had met other patients who had been hurled into the world of cancer treatment in hope of being healed or extending their lives. I met those who served at the American

Cancer Society and at specialty shops to help cancer survivors adjust to their new reality by assisting with wigs, prosthetics, specialty clothing, makeup, and other such needs. Most of these folks, just like the staff at Gabriel's House at Mayo, are typically cancer survivors who have found ways to give back by serving others on similar journeys.

This world of cancer is not by any means just pink. This just happens to be the color of the ribbon that symbolizes the type of cancer I had to face. Breast cancer is the number-two killer of women in the United States— just behind heart disease. It is gaining momentum now among younger women. The youngest person I've met with a diagnosis of breast cancer was twelve years old at the time she was diagnosed. This is inconceivable! We were once told that women should begin having annual mammograms at age forty unless they had a family history of breast cancer, in which case they should start screenings a little earlier. Now we see increasing numbers of women in their twenties and thirties being diagnosed, so waiting no longer makes sense to me. However, I know the experts have their reasons for telling women to wait. Then you have people like me. I had a clear mammogram, but the cancer had already been active and growing for months! Had I not returned to Dr. McCollum's office just to make sure the patch of bumpy skin I had discovered wasn't anything serious, I would not have been examined for another year. By that time, the cancer would have metastasized elsewhere in my body, and you would most likely not be reading these words today.

There are so many lives to save, so much to learn, so many people to encourage and support, and so much funding for research and educational programs to be secured. The need for *all* of the colorful worlds of cancer treatment, funding, and research is very real. We must fight for the funding for cancer research programs when they are put on the chopping block by the government. We must be the voice for those who are suffering from any type of cancer. I have not met a single person whose life has not been impacted either by his or her own cancer diagnosis or the diagnosis of a loved one. So for me, I now gladly enter the world of pink to do my part, to give back, to pay it forward, and to celebrate what I've overcome. I will eagerly embrace all opportunities to take what I've learned and use it to help someone else facing a similar journey.

To celebrate the end of a long eighteen months of cancer treatment, I chose to enter the Komen Race for the Cure, which was held in Knoxville in October 2012. Twelve of my closest friends and family joined me. I put together goodie bags for them. Each included a pink headband and water bottle along with some edible goodies and a personal letter expressing my deepest gratitude and love for each of them. Even my best friend, Linda, who lived in Arkansas, flew in to celebrate with me. We all met in downtown Knoxville's Market Square for dinner the night before the race. My friends made several connections that night, resulting in new friendships that continue to this day! Most of us spent that night at the Holiday Inn at Knoxville's World's Fair Park. That way we could just walk out the door into the sea of pink racers that would begin gathering there by 7:00 a.m. the next morning. My daughter made a sign that read, "Team Amy," and we made many pictures that Linda would later transform into a book for me. I could not imagine my heart being any more filled with love or feeling more blessed than I did on this weekend with my friends and family. We talked, walked, laughed, cried, hugged, took pictures, and reminisced. Every step I took amid the sea of pink on this 5K walk left me with a great sense of accomplishment. My husband joined us for lunch after the race, and he arrived with two dozen pink roses in his hand. It was the perfect ending to an unforgettable celebration.

What an incredible life I have been given, and now it includes the opportunity and responsibility to share with others what I've learned in hope of helping someone in some small way. I will continue to move forward with blood work every six months while taking what the Mayo oncologist called my "little dose of chemo," an aromatase inhibitor, every morning for a total of ten years. As I now move toward being a four-year cancer survivor, I am now truly honored and blessed to share with you the lessons I have learned while I was on this incredible journey.

Part 2

The Lessons Learned

Amy's daily devotional, Bible, and
first journal, titled *Dangling.*

Chapter 10

You Alone Cannot
Increase Your Faith

I learned very quickly that my faith in God was a gift from God himself. It was not the result of anything I had said or done. The development or growth of my faith did require my participation; however, the original seed of faith has been planted in our spirit by the one and only true God. Consider these verses. "Keeping our eyes on Jesus, the source and perfecter of our faith, who for the joy that lay before Him endured a cross and despised the shame and has sat down at the right hand of God's throne ... do not grow weary and lose heart" (Hebrews 12:2–3 HCSB). "For it is be grace you have been saved through faith—and this is not from yourselves, it is the gift of God—not by works, so that no one can boast" (Ephesians 2:8).

It was easy for me to accept the gift of salvation as a young child. I saw it just as that—a gift—for those willing to accept it. When we put our trust in Jesus Christ for our salvation, the seed of faith in Him is planted within us at that moment. For that faith

.trate our soul, (our mind, will, and emotions)
　　　 ꜱ affect our bodies, (what our mouth says, what
to ma⸍ do, and so on) will take time and will require our
w⸍ꜱss to surrender ourselves to the way and will of God.
⸍ this realization came the assurance that God wants that seed
⸍ faith He planted within me to grow, and as the gardener, He
will provide what is needed for such growth. My role is to trust,
obey, and abide in Him. Be it in a season of joy, a season of pain,
or both, God will be faithful to build the character of His Son in
us if we let Him.

God began to take me to Scriptures that led me down the path
of greater faith, a sustainable faith, and a faith beyond any measure
I had experienced before. I don't mean to imply that my life has
not included an active faith walk with God. I have stepped out
in faith many times before. However, I now needed my faith to
be much more than something I step out on in times of decision-
making or lean on when I've suffered a loss or disappointment.
I needed my faith in God and His goodness to pick me up and
carry me until I could stabilize my feet and point them in the
right direction toward greater faith, not greater fear. Verse after
verse, the Scriptures to which God led me began increasing my
understanding and my faith. A few of these included the following:

- Romans 3:28 (AMP) says, "For I am justified and made
  upright by faith independent of and distinctly apart from
  good deeds."
- Ephesians 3:12 (AMP) says, "Because of my faith in Him,
  I dare to have the boldness (courage and confidence) of
  free access to God with freedom and without fear."

- Ephesians 6:16 (AMP) says, "I lift up over all, the shield of faith, upon which I can quench all the flaming missiles of the wicked one."
- Hebrews 10:23 (HCSB) says, "I hold fast the confession of my hope without wavering for He who promised is faithful."

(Additional faith-focused Scriptures I often prayed aloud can be found in Appendix A.)

The Scriptures I most frequently focused on were James 1:2–3 and Proverbs 3:5–7. The passage from James explains that the "testing of your faith produces perseverance," which I would need for God to finish this work in my life, and the passage from the book of Proverbs instructs us to "trust in the Lord with all your heart and lean not on your own understanding, but in all your ways submit to him and He will make your paths straight. Do not be wise in your own eyes; fear the Lord and shun evil. This will bring health to your body and nourishment to your bones." Persevering for me not only meant physically enduring the treatment and surgeries. It meant standing firm in my faith, trading in my need for control and embracing true submission to God, and trusting Him to heal me in whatever manner He chose. More knowledge about this cancer or wisdom about how to eliminate it was not what I needed. The doctors were experts in this field and faced this dilemma many times. The burden of getting rid of cancer is on their shoulders, not mine! My job is to trust the Lord, shun evil by daily picking up my shield of faith, and persevere so that I can finish this race strong, mature, and lacking nothing. This requires deliberate action on my part to start my day in prayer, especially in those early morning hours when doubt and fear creep in even before I'm fully awake! *We must make up our minds every morning about who and what we're going to believe.*

Whether I am freed physically from this cancer temporarily or permanently is beyond my control. Satan loves to attack here because he knows how effective using fear in our lives is in crippling us, especially when we are facing the unknown or an unwanted known over which we have no power. I refused to let Satan gain this foothold in my life, no matter how hard he tried. I will live by faith, not by sight and not by what the world tells me. Remember the lepers Jesus healed? When He told them they were healed and directed them to go to the rabbi to be declared clean, they still had visible signs of leprosy all over their bodies. It wasn't until they began walking that journey with *faith* in what Jesus had told them—not in what they were seeing—that their healing began to manifest itself in their physical bodies. Jesus didn't want them walking away in faith dependent on what their eyes were seeing. He wanted them walking in faith dependent on Him as their Healer. So the Devil still had a few more arrows of doubt to hurl at me, but I too learned to focus on my dependence on God to increase my ability to walk by faith, not by sight. *He* is the author and perfecter of my faith. *He* is the giver and object of my faith, and *He* will increase my faith while strengthening my ability to walk in it. My obedience would be required, but my confidence in myself, in my strength, and in my understanding of the *why* behind what was happening would not be needed. I needed only to rest assured and *dangle*, knowing that God's plan was as perfect as His timing and that

He would finish the work He had startec
about to give up the solid ground beneath
I had finally left behind. My faith in th
challenged, but the result would be an e
relationship with God and feet of faith to stɩ
even greater challenges. As hymn writer Edw   ..ɩcu
it: "On Christ, the solid rock I stand, all other gɩound is sinking
sand, all other ground is sinking sand."

Pets just seem to know when you don't feel
well. Harley and Rusty are no exception.

Chapter 11

Intimacy with Christ Often Happens During a Crisis

Okay, so I've learned that adversity strengthens our faith, builds endurance, and increases our ability to stand under pressure. *God wants what is best for us, not what is easiest.* In my cries of desperation that the Lord would "let this cup of suffering be taken away from me," (Matthew 26:39, NLT), I realized He was sharing with me just a hint of what Jesus experienced in the garden of Gethsemane the night before His crucifixion. Revelation like this most often occurs during our times of brokenness, trials, and total dependence upon God. *Revelation in the midst of tragedy is divine favor!*

God uses trials to develop within us the character of His Son, Jesus. Crying out to God from my own despair for Him to intervene in my life gave me a deeper understanding from the inside out—not just mentally but with every fiber of my being—of what Jesus must have experienced that night in the Garden of Gethsemane. I began to understand a little more about the humanness that Jesus took on when He came to earth to save us.

My dear friend and Bible fellowship teacher Steve Loope can also testify to such intimacy with Christ. Steve unexpectedly lost his beloved wife of twenty-seven years and their only son within three weeks of each other. Most of us can never imagine the pain Steve has experienced or the trials he has faced in reconciling this adversity in his life. Steve will tell you that maintaining any sense of sanity or any desire to live on this earth another day in the face of such loss comes only by the grace of God, not out of any strength of his own. In his cries of desperation, our heavenly Father reached down and lifted Steve out of his despair. Steve shared with me his deeper understanding of how Peter must have felt when Jesus reached down and saved him from drowning. According to this story found in Matthew 14:25–32,

> The disciples were terrified when they saw Jesus walking the water toward their boat. Peter called out, "Lord, if it's you, tell me to come to you on the water." "Come" He said. "So Peter got down out of the boat, walked on the water and came toward Jesus. But when he saw the wind, he was afraid, and beginning to sink, cried out, "Lord Jesus, save me!" Immediately Jesus reached out his hand and caught him.

Now the disciples on the boat were blessed to witness this interaction between Jesus and Peter, but Peter *experienced* being personally rescued by the hand of God. After losing his wife and son, Steve also experienced the same loving, victorious, ever-present hand of God catching him and pulling him back from the brink of insanity. Steve understands the intimacy with Christ and divine revelation from God that can occur in the midst of great tribulation and loss.

Friends, do not resent trials and hardships in this life. Do not live to avoid such challenges. Trials and hardships are a very important part of your life! I have discovered that the most beautiful life is often the most broken life. The ashes from the death of what you thought would be may very well become the fertile soil from which a new life of victory will grow. God is forever covering each pain with His infinite love and mercy. He brings hope and encouragement where there was once only despair and death. Our faith in Him (not ourselves) to restore our lives is the key to reconciling adversity. The ability to see our situation as God sees it is divine favor shown to those who simply and sincerely ask for it. He is not the source of our wounds, but He is the healer of all that we trust into His hands. The beauty of this life is not reserved for only the mountaintop experiences with which we are blessed. *Remember: it is in the valley that the beautiful lilies grow!* You will find much beauty in the intimacy with Christ you experience when you totally surrender yourself and your circumstances to the one who created you and knows you best. This goes against our human tendencies of wanting to be in control and wanting to fix the problem so we can be freed from the hardship we are experiencing, but it can be done. None of us likes pain. None of us enjoy waiting for answers or not being in control, but by enduring trials, we develop patience, which produces perseverance, a stronger faith, and a closeness with God that we may not otherwise ever develop.

The Chilhowee Hills Celebration Choir praying
over Amy before going out to sing.

Amy debuting "Trust," written by minister of worship
David Stewart, who is seen in the background.

Chapter 12

Be Authentic, Real, and Transparent

A diagnosis of cancer is incredibly scary and life-altering. The feeling of vulnerability it creates is instant and constant. My automatic response to this news was to reach out to my family and closest friends because I knew I did not want to face this giant alone. I assumed most if not everyone would agree that this was not something for anyone to face alone. I soon discovered that some people would do anything to keep others from knowing they had been diagnosed with cancer. They had responded by choosing seclusion and maintaining as much privacy as possible. This realization made me stop and evaluate my decision to share with others what I was going through. It made me question my decision to sometimes wear bandanas, ball caps, and scarves, given that this was a sure confirmation to those who saw me that I was battling some type of cancer. If I wore a wig every day, however, there was a good chance others would not know.

As I mentioned earlier, even though cancer is rooted in a problem within our physical bodies, our ability to live victoriously while coping with it goes far beyond the physical realm. We must respond mentally, spiritually, and emotionally as well. I was keenly aware that I was on display. Others would be watching me as I walked through this fire to see if my walk matched my talk—and I've talked a lot over the years! I was raised in a Christian home with godly parents, and I have attended church all of my life. I married a godly man. We've raised our children in a Christian home, and most if not all who know me know I have preached "walk what you talk" for many years. I have also encouraged my children to live with nothing to hide, nothing to fear, nothing to prove, and nothing to regret. Now I felt as if a huge spotlight from heaven was shining down on me for all to see how I was going to respond to this attack on my life. Would I live by the same standard I had held for my children? Would mine be a walk of faith or one of fear? I chose to be authentic. *By authentic I mean real, the truest version of me that I could be, inside and out.*

From day one of my cancer journey, I began to glean from other cancer patients and survivors vital nuggets of wisdom that helped me successfully maneuver through my own treatment voyage. I would have not received the blessing of their help had they chosen seclusion or their own privacy over the opportunity to encourage someone else by sharing their experiences. I also did not have the time or energy to worry about what others thought about how I looked or what I should or should not be doing. My main desire was for others to see my faith had feet. My sole responsibility was to honor Christ while on this journey and obey Him regardless of what the future might hold. He allowed me to travel this road for a reason, and my focus had to be solely on Him if I was going to fulfill His purpose for my trial.

In this kind of faith walk, feelings of fear, doubt, and vulnerability become consistent, unwanted companions. I felt vulnerable when I first asked my pastors to anoint me with oil and pray over me, but this act of obedience left me with the very peace of God "that transcends all understanding" (Philippians 4:7). While they were praying over me, Pastor David Stewart was inspired to write a song based on Proverbs 3:5–6, which Pastor Mark McKeehan read out loud just before they began praying for me. David immediately began arranging his new original song, which he titled "Trust," and within the week he and Josh Lovelace (of the band Need to Breathe) played it for me. We began planning when I could sing it along with the choir. This experience was pivotal in my walk with the Lord. Though I didn't choose seclusion while I was going through cancer treatment, I wasn't sure how I felt about singing on stage with no hair, in a scarf, and in the middle of chemo. What kind of sane person would commit to that? We strategically set a date for me to sing toward the end of one of my chemo cycles just before starting the next one so that my strength would be optimal.

As I mentioned earlier, the women in the choir wore scarves on their heads, and the men wore pink shirts or ties to show their support. I helped tie the scarves for several women that morning before the sound check. The choir prayed over me just before we went out. The love and unity experienced by this team of worship leaders was indescribable. Pastor Mark explained to the congregation that I was going through cancer treatment and that the choir was dressed in pink to show their support for me. He veryone that I was about to sing the song that Pastor inspired to write during our prayer time together a months earlier. I had about thirty family members in the congregation who came to support me that day.

While I will admit I was nervous, I was also very aware that this moment in time—this instance of me being me and singing in the middle of this storm—would most likely never be repeated but would forever change my life. All the doubt that said, "I can't do this. I shouldn't do this. People just don't do this," melted away as I began to sing the words of Proverbs 3:5–6, "Trust in the Lord with all your heart, lean not on your understanding. In all your ways, acknowledge him, and he will direct your path."

Talk about a battle between fear and faith! This wasn't about me being some great vocalist. This was about me being transparent in my worship and not letting fear rob from me a moment that God had ordained as mine. I will forever be grateful for Pastor David and his desire to lead others to experience true, raw, authentic worship. The phrase "sacrifice of praise" now has a new meaning for me, and I am forever changed!

Choosing to be authentic carried many different meanings as I continued on through treatment. Regardless of the situation, I believed that being the best version of me was the only way to respond. Had I not gone shopping in my bandanas and ball caps, I would never have experienced the encouragement of other cancer survivors who knew *the look* and chose to reach out to me. I will never forget their stories, and their impact on my life will last forever. I felt vulnerable the first time I called together my closest coworkers and supervisors to tell them of my diagnosis. I shared with them the anchor Scriptures on which I would rely for strength to carry on, which, of course, included continuing to take care of my work responsibilities. Had I not, I would never have known the willingness of my coworkers to help and support me as I continued to work while going through treatment. My regional director allowed me to work as much as possible from home. When I made long trips to another county, my husband would sometimes put on his chauffeur's hat and drive me around. My relationships with my coworkers, some with whom I have worked for almost twenty years, were strengthened even more as they walked beside me on this journey.

The first time I attended church with a scarf on my head, especially since I sit on the front row of the choir, was very intimidating, but had I not done it, I would never have known the incredible love, support, and compassion that my church family extended to me. Had I not shared my darkest moments and greatest fears with my husband, I would not have experienced the deeper intimacy that we now share because we faced this trial together. I could share for hours the countless stories of the blessings I have received from being *real* and letting others walk this road with me regardless of the twists and turns we faced.

I admit, though, some moments of being true to myself were very challenging. Sometimes it meant asking for or extending forgiveness so that closeness and freedom in a relationship could be restored. Some moments involved making others aware of how their words or actions negatively affected me or someone in my family. Some days being authentic meant letting the tears flow, while other days it meant laughing in the midst of extreme, life-altering situations. Sometimes it meant sitting in complete silence while my husband held me in his arms, tears rolling down our faces. The day he cut my hair, it meant joking over dinner with my family to make sure none of my hair had fallen onto their dinner plates! Being the best version of me has also meant surrendering my guilt for being unable to meet others' needs and instead accepting their help for a while. Again, this is tough for those of us who like to be in charge!

On one particular day, just being me meant excusing myself from visiting with a friend so I could go throw up in the kitchen trash can before returning to the conversation. It meant facing the world with no hair, eyelashes, or eyebrows. Being me after surgery meant being completely dependent on my husband to help me sit up, stand, walk, or empty my drains. Being real meant going out in public with no prosthetics because my chest was simply too burned from the radiation to wear them. Being true to myself also meant celebrating the end of treatment with my closest friends and relatives by walking in the Komen Race for a Cure with a great sense of accomplishment along with pride, sincere love, and appreciation for all who stuck by me!

Here is the best advice I can give a cancer warrior in this arena of being authentic. Don't look for the reasons to avoid engaging with others while going through treatment! *Look for the blessings that come with allowing others into your world despite your fear or feeling of vulnerability.* Avoid the trap of feeling like you have to feel well enough to put on makeup or clean up the house before having a friend over. Don't worry about what other people think about your wig or bandanas or if they'll notice your dirty dishes in the sink. Not only will others bless and encourage you on your journey, but you will inspire them to be authentic and courageous as well! Who benefits if we wear masks and pretend to be something we're not? Being real doesn't give you a license to start complaining, blaming, or whining about your circumstances. It means choosing to control what you can in a way that shows those around you that you are not defeated, you are not wasting time worrying and doubting, and most of all, you are not dead yet! You are more than a conqueror. You are stronger than you think! The blessings and freedom that come from being the truest version of *you* not only makes your life more livable but inspires others to be real too. I want real relationships where unconditional love and acceptance abound! Don't you?

Amy with her husband, David, who was very
instrumental in helping her guard her heart and mind.

Chapter 13

Guard Your Heart, Eyes, Ears, Mind, Everything!

You will be amazed at all that you hear and see while going through cancer treatment. It is vital that you not be led astray by well-meaning people. One day when I was shopping for a wig, the lady helping me felt the need to tell me a horror story about her friend who was also fighting breast cancer. Her diagnosis was very similar to mine. She went on to tell me all the details of her friend's struggles and how she would never be cured from her disease. She added that she had once been a nurse and believed that most breast cancers, once they've reached stage three or four, are incurable. There I sat, stuck in her presence as she placed a variety of wigs on my head, trying to find a way out.

Another lady I've known about five years saw me out one day and asked me if I was wearing the bandana because I was sick. I replied that I was undergoing chemotherapy, and she responded, "You know cancer can spread in between chemo treatments, right?" Once again, I started looking for the door. When I asked her why she felt she needed to tell me this, she responded that I needed to know for my own good. Trust me. This did not help me either.

Some folks mean well when they tell you stories and some are simply not able to put themselves in your shoes. Some want to share how their lives have been touched by cancer. Some don't know what to say, but in their effort to connect with you, they end up sharing too much about someone else's cancer journey. I would encourage others to stick with admitting they don't know what to say! You're not alone! Most of us don't!

Some people are insensitive out of ignorance, while some just need to think another minute before they speak. Even the innocent response, "Oh, I'm so sorry," can hit like a rock. At times I had to convince others that I was going to be okay, while they gave me reasons why I might not be okay. Is that not crazy? Most people do not mean to harm you in any way, but they will walk away never realizing the impact of their words. Don't become angry or bitter. Just realize your role in redirecting those talking to you when needed.

It is incumbent upon you to stand guard over your mind and heart. It is your job to base your view of your situation on what you know to be true, not on what you fear could be true. Satan will use anything and anybody to keep the feelings of doubt and fear alive in your soul. For example, I met a woman in the chemo center one day, and she was literally gone the next week. She was younger than me and was diagnosed with a totally different cancer that was further progressed than mine, but the realization of her death attacked my hope and confidence in my healing.

I learned to hold tightly to what God's Word says about me and the future and hope that God has for me, not the fear I saw in others' eyes or in the stories they shared. I focused on what my doctor told me about my prognosis, not what others thought it could be. At one point my husband had to call the oncology nurse to help me clarify something someone had said to me. The nurse read every word of Dr. Ibach's dictation to David so he could be assured, and could thus reassure me, that what this person had said to me about the type of cancer I had was not true. Some folks just do not have a filter when talking to others, so I try to overlook it because this issue probably affects all areas of their lives. We could all stand to talk a little less. *Sensitivity doesn't just happen. It's learned.* Because I have been on the receiving end of cancer, I have learned that what often brings comfort requires fewer words than most think. I just needed people to be by my side, to pray for me, to ask how my day was going, to treat me like they would anyone else. I'm not saying that acknowledging my situation was either unwarranted or unappreciated, but I did not want others to feel it had to be the sole topic of our conversations. I wanted to talk about the weather, family, how work was going, what was for dinner, and other everyday topics.

Of course, I confided in my closest family and friends when I needed encouragement and some of them experienced some of my toughest days with me. I would never recommend going through this alone. Instead I recommend that you just be prepared to divert your attention quickly away from any potential snares that may arise through the well-meaning words of others. Stay focused on your specific journey and who is in charge of it. Be assertive when necessary. Ask people to change the subject of your conversation. Let them know when something they've said stirs up pain or fear within you. This is how we learn from one another. In my next book, I will include direct quotes from cancer patients regarding what has been most helpful to them in getting through their cancer journey. I think this will be helpful to all of us as we learn to comfort others we care about.

Amy with her best friend, Linda, who traveled from
Arkansas to see her. She also gave Amy an actual
rearview mirror for Christmas to remind her that
in God's time line, she's already been healed.

Chapter 14

Rearview Mirror Theology

I had not thought about this concept before I was introduced to a cancer patient named Marvella on my first day in the chemo room. Marvella had been fighting cancer for quite a while. She was a petite, feisty, African-American woman who appeared to be perhaps in her mid sixties. Marvella had obviously decided to be an encouragement to whomever she met. She talked with me and David while we were sitting through my very first chemo. I'll never forget the intensity and intentionality of her advice to me.

She started, "Now, Amy, let me tell you something, honey. You do *not* own this cancer, so don't talk like you do."

Slightly confused, I asked what she meant. She went on to explain that I shouldn't say, "*My* cancer is this or that," or, "The doctors are treating *my* cancer with this or that."

"No! No! No!" she said.

I told her how I had already told the choir before I was diagnosed that whatever was invading my body was not welcome and that I was ready to fight it.

She said, "Exactly, Amy! You are to claim only what is of God. You can say that the doctors have diagnosed you with a type of cancer, but do not make it your own, like it's going to stay with you. Whether you are temporarily healed now or eternally healed in heaven, you will be healed either way!"

I'm so glad I learned early on *not* to claim ownership over this cancer. The connection between what we believe and speak impacts the road to healing! *We must walk in faith of what we know to be true, not in fear of what we don't know or can't control.* As I mentioned earlier, we must decide each day who and what we're going to believe. I believed I was being healed and that God's plan for me was still good and his timing, perfect.

Marvella also reminded me of the story of Jesus healing the ten lepers that I've already mentioned in chapter 10, but I believe it's worthy of a closer look.

> Now, on his way to Jerusalem, Jesus traveled along the border between Samaria and Galilee. As he was going into a village, ten men who had leprosy met him. They stood at a distance and called out in a loud voice, "Jesus, Master, have pity on us!" When he saw them, he said, "Go, show yourselves to the priests." And *as they went,* they were cleansed. One of them, when he saw he was healed, came back, praising God in a loud voice. He threw himself at Jesus' feet and thanked him—and he was a Samaritan. Jesus asked, "Were not all ten cleansed? Where are the other nine? Has no one returned to give praise to God except this foreigner?" Then he said to him, "Rise and go; your faith has made you well." (Luke 17:11–17)

These men knew Jesus was the Son of God and had the power to heal them. Not only did they believe it, but they acted upon it and called out to Him to have mercy on them. When He saw them, He instructed them to go to the priest to be declared clean. Now were they healed? Yes, I believe they were instantly healed. Had that healing manifested in their bodies in an observable way? No, they couldn't see the healing until they obeyed God's command to go. Look at it! Verse 14 says, "As they went, they were cleansed." Not before they went but *as they went.*

Those lepers walked toward the rabbi so that he could declare them clean out of *obedience* to Christ and in *faith* of what He had already done, not because of what they saw or felt. Marvella then declared, "Amy, your healing has already come. You only have to walk it out in faith by coming in here and doing whatever the doctors that the Lord has chosen for you tell you to do."

Out of this understanding came the rearview mirror theology that my husband often used to keep us both moving forward. We could keep walking toward the future God had for us because of the confidence we had in the work He has already done for us and in us! I knew my faith and obedience were key to living a victorious life, even when what was before me felt incredibly daunting or overwhelming. I would get snagged again by fear—when I was told I needed a second six-month round of chemo—but David would just hold me and whisper in my ear, "Rearview mirror, baby! In God's time line, you're already healed."

I knew I wanted truly to walk in victory despite what my situation looked like, and I wanted to inspire those walking with me to do the same. I wanted to be like the Samaritan and give thanks and praise to God for my healing. The story of the lepers became an anchor that not only held me through tough times during treatment but would help me face trying times in the future too. No matter what I'm facing, I look at an actual rearview mirror with one of my anchor verses written on it—a Christmas gift from my best friend—and I think, *This is already accomplished in God's time line. Just walk it out in faith. Rearview mirror, baby. rearview mirror!*

Amy singing with the Chilhowee Hills Celebration Choir at Knoxville's World's Fair Park. This is one of three concerts she participated in while she was going through her first six months of chemo.

Amy singing with her dad at Pleasant Hill United Methodist Church, where Amy was raised. Her parents have been members of this church nearly their entire lives, and Amy is close to many members there.

Chapter 15

Open Your Mouth!

The best way to stop wrong thinking is to open your mouth and speak what is right. I believe we should avoid talking about what we *don't* want in our lives and focus on what we *do* want! I encourage you to speak words of praise and words of faith regardless of your circumstance. Second Corinthians 10:5 says, "We demolish arguments and every pretension that sets itself up against the knowledge of God, and we take captive every thought to make it obedient to Christ." To stop unwanted thoughts, we must counteract them by speaking what we want our brain to think more readily on its own. We must talk less about our situation and more about what we want to come to pass! I look in the mirror and declare out loud, "I'm the healthiest fifty-year-old I know!"

Fear, doubt, and confusion are among the most dangerous and deceptive tools Satan uses to keep us from living the abundant life that Christ died for us to live. Satan is real, and he is the Great Deceiver and Father of Lies. He preys on us when we are vulnerable in an attempt to destroy us, usually from the inside out, by attacking our emotions and our thoughts. He attacks us through situations, other people (sometimes even well-meaning people), what we think, and what we see. He cannot rob us of our position in Christ as an overcomer, but he can convince us—if we let him—that we are defeated. First John 4:4 promises, "You dear children are from God and have overcome them, because the One who is in you is greater than the one who is in the world." In context, this passage encourages us to "test the spirits to determine if they are from God" (1 John 4:1 HCSB). With God's help, we can know what is of God and what is of Satan. Any spirit that does not acknowledge Jesus Christ is the Son of God is of the world and does not hold the power of Christ to overcome evil.

Overcome thoughts of defeat by meditating on and speaking out loud the truths of God! Hebrews 10:23 (HCSB) encourages us, "Let us hold fast the *confession* of our hope without wavering, for He who promised is faithful." I will never stop speaking of the hope I have because of what Christ has done for me. Cancer cannot take that away from me! Nothing can separate me from the love of God! *Hallelujah!* The Lord's declaration in Jeremiah 29:11 is also reassuring. "For I know the plans I have for you, declares the Lord, plans to prosper you and not to harm you, to give you a hope and a future." Give the Devil a dose of that when he comes calling! He is powerless! I know it is difficult to trust in God's plan for your life when you are in the middle of a trial. We must learn to look through the circumstances to see how God can use our situations to grow and strengthen us or those around us who are witnessing what we're experiencing.

As believers, we can trust Roman 8:28, which says, "And we know that in all things God works for the good of those who love

Him, who have been called according to his purpose." unknown to us is not unknown to God, and what Satan m to use for our destruction, God will use for our sanctification! Psalm 27:1 asks, "The LORD is my Light and Salvation, whom shall I fear or dread? The Lord is the Refuge and Stronghold of my life, of whom shall I be afraid?" You must remember that Satan is a defeated foe! He has no power over you, your soul, your body, or your spirit! We are reminded in Romans 8:37 (HCSB), "Yet amid all these things we are more than conquerors and gain a surpassing victory through Him who loved us." Keep these verses at your fingertips, and repeat them often! Keeping my mind focused on the truths of God was vital to my rising above the daily attacks on my mind while going through cancer treatment. We must always be on guard and quick to counteract deceptive thoughts by speaking aloud God's promises as well as His truths and confirming our trust in His power! If you can worry, you can meditate! The more we meditate on God's Word and verbalize His promises, the more readily our brain will access these truths when we need them, thus leading us to stay on the path of the overcomer! The Devil is indeed defeated! We, however, are not, so open your mouth and tell him so!

I didn't realize the palm tree was in need
of pruning, but the gardener knew. So
it is with our heavenly Father.

Chapter 16

Palm Tree Revelation

In June 2011, during my first six-month round of chemo, we went on vacation with my parents. This trip to the beach was like no other. Instead of lounging in the sun, I spent a great deal of time resting and reflecting under a tent, fully clothed, out of the harmful rays of the sun. I was very thankful just to be there, to have the chance to watch people come and go, and to get away from the so-called "real world" for a while.

I will never forget something the Lord revealed to me on this trip. David and I were sitting on the balcony of our condo when we noticed a palm tree by the pool. How beautiful and full it was! The very next day, we noticed it again. Much to my surprise, it had been pruned. Dead branches were lying on the ground all around it. It struck me that I was in the process of being pruned as well! In John 15:1, Jesus says, "I am the true vine, and my Father is the gardener. He cuts off every branch in me that bears no fruit, while every branch that does bear fruit he prunes so that it will be even more fruitful."

We had not noticed the branches of the palm tree that had turned brown and were no longer contributing to the beauty of the tree, but what wasn't obvious to us was obvious and significant to the gardener. So it is with our lives. So many people have commented to me, "You are so strong," or, "You are such an inspiration," but they had no idea of the spiritual warfare raging within me. When I saw that palm tree transformed into a new, even more beautiful creation the next day, I knew God was doing this in my life as well. What was being cut off or pruned within me was not obvious to those around me; however, I knew, and so did God.

I looked at those brown, decaying branches lying on the ground and thought to myself, *Lord, there lie my doubt, my fear, my worry, my self-pity, my indifference, my excuses, my blinders, and everything else that has kept me from living the abundant life You died for me to live. Take them all!* What a revelation! I'll warmly reflect on this moment every time I see a palm tree for the rest of my life!

John 15: 3–5 (ESV) says,

> You are already clean because of the word I have spoken to you. Abide in me, and I in you. As the branch cannot bear fruit by itself, unless it abides in the vine, neither can you, unless you abide in me. I am the vine; you are the branches. Whoever abides in me and I in him, he it is that bears much fruit, for apart from me you can do nothing.

In those moments that I have chosen to truly trust God with my decisions and circumstances, He has been honored, and I have been blessed in return. However, this should not be an occasional experience or one linked only to the major decision-making times in my life, but rather it should be the *pattern* of my life.

Until I learn to *abide* in Christ and His Word, until it's a part of my everyday experience, I will not bear the fruit I am meant to bear. He is taking away parts of me that are not bearing fruit and gently pruning back the parts of me that are so that I may bear *more* fruit through a life lived fully in compliance with His plan and not my own. Love, peace, joy, goodness, patience, self control, and kindness—these are not just to be experienced or expressed in the good days of life but *every* day and even in the midst of adversity! "How?" you may ask. By *abiding* in the Holy Spirit and in God's Word. When we are saved, we are given the presence of the Holy Spirit, the Counselor, who imparts all the wisdom and guidance we need when we ask. We must learn to listen to the Spirit of God and to follow His direction in all things, big and small. We must also learn to discern what is of God and what is not. We must do more than just read the Bible. We must study it, meditate on it, and hide its truths in our hearts so that we may draw upon those truths every day of our lives.

Abiding means permanent, long-lasting, enduring, unshakable, and steadfast. Friends, abiding takes deliberate effort, practice, and commitment. Prior to my cancer journey, if you had asked me if I walked in faith and trusted God, I would have answered yes. However, spending time in prayer and in studying the Word so that I could truly abide in Him on a daily basis in *all* circumstances is something I have not yet mastered. The more I abide in Him, the more He can do through me. The more I am in step with His plan, the more His plan is at work in me, creating the desires of my heart that He wants me to have. The world will tell me that my security is in my ability to take what's mine, to be in control, and to pursue money and possessions. But I know better, and now I have palm tree revelation! It is in letting go of such desires and pursuing a closer relationship with Christ that true security and freedom is found.

As God continues to purge unfruitful attitudes and actions from my life, my prayer is that you will begin to see a new creation emerge—one like the palm tree on the second day. I pray that you see more of *Christ in me* than you see *of me*. I want the fruit of my life to be that of true joy, patience, kindness, self-control, and peace on a daily basis regardless of any circumstance I may face.

God uses all kinds of people and situations to test our faith and help us grow in our ability to abide in Him. Don't get stuck grieving the death of an old way of life, for a new beautiful life may be emerging out of its ashes. While the familiarity of your old life may bring you comfort, God is a God of new beginnings! Second Corinthians 5:17 tells us, "Therefore if any man be in Christ, he is a new creature, old things have passed away; behold all things have become new." God is doing a new work in you! When I first realized God was not showing me how to die but how to truly live, I knew I had to let go of some attitudes and habits in order to take hold of the new life God was leading me to live. Sometimes this was easy, and I would welcome the change with open arms. Other times change was much more difficult, but Philippians 1:6 says, "I am confident of this, that

He who began a good work in you will carry it on to completion until the day of Christ Jesus." God will not lead us where He does not sustain us. Abide in Him so that your dependence is on His power, not your own, for it is only through His strength that all things are possible!

Amy with her pink boxing gloves that her friend
Mary Anna sent her from Chattanooga.

Mary Anna with her pink boxing gloves. She was
diagnosed with breast cancer soon after Amy.

Chapter 17

A Time to Endure

Waiting for news, for direction, for confirmation, for relief, or for anything can be challenging. It can be especially difficult when we know God could take away our pain and suffering with a blink of His eye. So why does He linger? Why is His timing so different from ours? Because He desires to test our faith, teach us patience, and strengthen our ability to persevere. In other words, He wants to make us more like Jesus. *Patience is a fruit of the Spirit that only is developed through trials.* According to Hebrews 6:12 (NASB), both faith and patience are required for us to receive the promises of God. It reads "so that you won't be sluggish, but imitators of those who through faith and patience inherit the promises." Paul didn't pray for the church's problems to go away, but he prayed that they could *endure* whatever came with good temper.

According to Exodus 13:17, God purposely led the Israelites the long way through the desert because in taking the shorter route, they would have engaged their enemies before they were ready. To reach the Promised Land, they would have to depend completely on God while they fought many wars and endured much hardship. God first had to deal with their weaknesses, doubts and complaining. The Israelites quickly became disgruntled with Moses and wanted to return to Egypt—to what was *known*, even though it meant slavery. Why? Because they felt comfort in what was known even if it was not best. They focused on their problem, not their problem solver! They feared the unknown, and doubt filled their minds and hearts. How could they move forward into battle with such fear? They couldn't. Only by developing complete dependence on God (and not themselves) did their faith and courage grow.

Have you ever allowed fear of the unknown to keep you from doing something you knew God was leading you to do? God may be preparing you to face the struggles you may encounter as He brings you to a new way of living. Trust me. The second you set your sights on doing anything for God, the Enemy is aware and ready to attack. But don't lose heart! Remember: "Blessed is the one who perseveres under trial because, having stood the test, that person will receive the crown of life that the Lord has promised to those who love him" (James 1:12).

This also brings us back to Proverbs 3:5–6. We've all heard it, right? At the risk of redundancy, let's take one last look at verse 5, which says, "Trust in the Lord with all your heart, and lean not on your understanding. In all your ways acknowledge Him, and He will make your paths straight." Don't just think it. Say it! Don't just say it. Walk it! Stop trying to figure out the trial you're facing. Stop trying to fix what is beyond your control to fix! Again, what is unknown to you is never unknown to God, and if you will trust Him—surrender all that you are to all that He is— He will direct your steps and see you through. When the attacks of fear, doubt, confusion, and fatigue come upon you, rest in the fact that the one attacking you is already defeated! He has *no* power over you! Even if your mind is tired and you're not thinking clearly, go to the promises and truths of God and say them out loud until you no longer hear the enemy taunting you. God will hear you, and He will rescue you, comfort you, and restore your peace of mind.

We equip ourselves for these attacks by putting on the full armor of God. What many of us learned as a child, perhaps in VBS or Sunday school, we must now apply to our lives. Ephesians 6:11-18 instructs us,

> Put on the full armor of God, so that you can take your *stand against the devil's schemes*. For our struggle is not against flesh and blood, but against the rulers, against the authorities, against the powers of this dark world and against the spiritual forces of evil in the heavenly realms. Therefore put on the full armor of God, so that when the day of evil comes, you may be able to *stand your ground*, and after you have done everything, *to stand*. *Stand firm* then, with the belt of truth buckled around your waist, with the breastplate of righteousness in place, and with your feet fitted with the readiness that comes from the gospel of peace. In addition to all this, take up the shield of faith, with which you can extinguish all the flaming arrows of the evil one. Take the helmet of salvation and the sword of the Spirit, which is the word of God.

Did you notice that the word *stand* was used in this passage four times? Our ability to stand is often strengthened through adversity. I once told Steve Loope that my desire was not only to "stand" during this trial but to "stand well." I knew that trying to endure a spiritual battle—such as one that accompanies a physical attack like cancer—with anything other than the armor of God would only bring me failure. Many times when I would *dangle*, I would picture myself curled up in the right hand of God Himself, my shield of faith covering my body. Other times I took out my sword of the Spirit, my Bible, and meditated on God's promises, which I knew would extinguish anything that was attempting to overwhelm or deceive me. I stood firm in the truth of God's promises, ignoring the lies the enemy whispered in my ear. The more experience we gain using this armor of God, the more natural it will become, and the more quickly we will defeat the spiritual forces of evil that try to overtake us. Our ability to gain victory over battles fought in the spiritual realm directly affects our ability to experience victory over battles fought in the physical realm, regardless of what they may be.

Amy retired in June 2014 after working twenty-eight years as a social worker, and David retired in January 2013 after an eighteen-year career in real estate preceded by another twelve years of working in sales. They now enjoy spending time on the beautiful lakes of East Tennessee, movie nights with their kids, camping, spontaneous weekend getaways, and of course, Tennessee football.

Chapter 18

Life beyond the Grip of Cancer

A life well lived is the best revenge against cancer.

—Anonymous

Survivors don't simply stop fighting after treatment is over. A battle still rages in our souls and spirits, and we deal with it daily. We don't often discuss this battle because we won't let it occupy our precious time and energy. We can't give in to fear, doubt, or deception from the enemy who wants to use our situations to keep us from living life to the fullest. The same is true for those who have lost people precious to them to cancer. By pressing on and living the life God has for you, after saying good-bye for now to the ones you love, you are also claiming victory over cancer every day. Our sweet loved ones have received their ultimate and eternal healing. Cancer has no hold on them. Nor will it blind or bind us, because we will be overcomers again ... and again ... and again.

Yes, we have many scars—physically, emotionally, and mentally—but they all remind us of where we've been, what tried to hurt us, and what we've defeated. *Scars cannot dictate where we're going, but they do reflect what we've overcome on our way to getting there.* Think of Jesus' scarred hands and feet! They do not reflect wounds that kept Him from defeating death. His body bears them because He did defeat death! He showed them to others, like Thomas, to dispel any doubt that He had indeed conquered death so that they too could live with Him forever. Our struggles on this earth are nothing compared to the crucified life of Christ, but through our trials He teaches us lessons that parallel those He taught while here on earth. Yes, we've been wounded, but we will stand. We still endure. Our scars are evidence that we are indeed overcomers of all that has tried to keep us from living the life that Christ died for us to live! The cross could not hold Him. The grave could not keep Him. The Pharisees could not explain Him away. Sin could not bind Him. Evil could not deter Him from his mission, and nothing of this world can separate us from Him!

The hope that will carry us into our future after cancer is not faith in ourselves or what we can do but faith in God's grace and what He will do through us. Our peace isn't of our own making. The world can't soothe our weary souls when the fear of a recurrence fills our hearts and minds. This fear sends us reeling back to our anchor, our source of strength in times of trouble, our bedrock, our cornerstone, the one who holds healing in His hands, the only one who knows our future—Jesus Christ. Until He returns or calls us home, we trust in His timing, purpose, love, faithfulness, and grace. We lay at His feet our attempts to control that over which we truly have no control, knowing that His plan for us, whatever it may be, is perfect. We meditate on His Word and are reminded that freedom comes with surrender. We ask Him to prepare us for whatever lies ahead and to give us strength to endure whatever it may be. We ask for His peace to dwell in our hearts every day and for the ability to trust Him completely with our lives, and we walk forward with faith in His ability to care for us.

This way of life plays out daily, not just in obviously spiritual ways but in the very ordinary, simple, day-to-day decisions we make. *We don't walk away from our experience with cancer the same as we entered into it.* We have been reminded of the fragility of life and the need to draw every ounce of joy from it while we can. We become more sensitive to what really matters in life. Little things don't bother us anymore. Disruptions no longer needlessly frustrate us. Complaining decreases, and the need to find the best in every situation increases. This new life is not a life of denial but a life of gratitude. We don't want our time spent with those we love to be wasted on arguing or talking about things that simply don't matter. We no longer want to focus on gaining things that carry no eternal value. We want our energy going toward making a positive impact on the lives of those we love. We want to spend more time with them, laugh with them, and enjoy living with them. We want to share the invaluable lessons that we've learned with anyone who will listen to us. Others' views, criticisms, or judgments of us just don't carry the weight that perhaps they once did. We value the relationships in our lives that are based on authenticity. We don't have time to appease others, put on appearances, or impress anyone. We focus less on being right and more on being righteous. We want to honor God with our lives because the reality that He has spared us, healed us, and restored us is ever-present in the forefront of our minds. We want to take care of our bodies and want the best out of life, and we are willing to fight for it.

Don't feel sorrow or pity for us. Look at us with envy. We have learned lessons that have greatly altered our lives and enabled us to see life with a completely new, incredibly powerful perspective. We can find joy in the most mundane, disliked daily responsibilities ever! We are content when others wring their hands in worry, and we are full of hope when the media says there is none. This perspective keeps us humble, grateful, and sensitive to others. We are able to keep our priorities straight with much less effort than ever before. We see what matters most much more clearly and easily. While cancer is an ugly, unfair, unwanted part of our life story, we have managed to draw every ounce of goodness that comes with such a journey and the victory over this disease. Wounded? Sure. Defeated? Not a chance.

We live in a fallen, corrupt, hurting world, and cancer is unfortunately a part of that; however, we cannot live in fear of it or anything else that comes with living in such a world. It's worth repeating that the Devil cannot prophesy our life, nor can he prophesy our death. God alone has numbered our days. My dad in his wisdom once told me, "We can't control how many days we have on this earth, but what we can control is how we live them." Therefore, we must be the carriers of hope, faith, joy, contentment, love, gratitude, conviction, commitment, and perseverance. *Cancer doesn't define us or our destiny.* It has simply provided us with a launch pad from which we now can soar ahead with a new determination to live life to the fullest. We now have clearer vision, greater purpose, freedom, and the power of experience and revelation to help us impact others for the better. For this new perspective and the experience of learning how to *dangle*, I will always be inexpressibly grateful!

Appendix A

Help for the Soul and Spirit

At the onset of my cancer journey, I was ambushed by the spiritual warfare that came with it. When I began to search the Scriptures for help and direction, I found the following verses to be incredibly powerful in setting my path straight and counteracting the fear and doubt that flooded my heart and mind. *Dangling* is simply how I describe the visualization of me resting in the protection and victory found only in God's righteous right hand. Dangling is about trusting His hold on me, not my hold on Him. It's deliberately taking time alone to focus on His promises to me, His love for me, and His protection of me. Meditating on these verses has been a vital part of this life-changing perspective. I hope that you find these verses just as helpful as you fight the battles you are facing. Keep this quick Scripture reference within reach.

Second Corinthians 10:4 reveals, "The weapons of our warfare are not carnal, but mighty in God for pulling down strongholds." There is more to living this life than what you see, what you can explain, or what you control. We are spiritual beings having a physical experience, not mere physical beings having a spiritual experience. Our struggle to endure the trials of this world, to experience emotions without letting them control us, and to keep a sound mind and peace in our hearts is spiritual, not physical. This is why Jesus sent the Holy Spirit to us—to minister to us in our *spirit*, which is eternal, while our physical bodies are only temporary. In your spirit God will minister to you and destroy any stronghold in your life that keeps you from living the astounding life He wants you to live!

The Bible is alive, and it contains all the truths and promises of God for all of us. Some people think they can't understand the Bible, so they never pick it up. Why would God inspire people to write down such power for generations to come in a way that we could never understand? *He didn't.* He teaches us through His Word how to live a life of freedom, power, and joy! Don't be deceived into thinking the Bible is too big, too complicated, or too hard to comprehend or apply to your life. *It's not!* Countless Bible studies and guides are available to help you study one specific topic or one book of the Bible at a time! You just have to break it down. Don't you eat a meal one bite at a time? So it is with studying God's Word. Christians, don't become apathetic or content with only a Sunday morning's dose of Scripture. Life and power are in these words!

I'm not a coffee drinker, but I know many people say they could not live without their morning coffee. Some say, "Don't even talk to me until I've had my coffee!" *Having your quiet time with God and drinking in the power of His Word will set your day straighter than any cup of coffee ever could.* Let it infiltrate your mind and heart so you can see your world the way God sees it! See *yourself* as God sees you! Let the Holy Spirit minister to you through the His Word. This will change your entire perspective on your life. Worry will become a thing of the past. Doubt, uncertainty, and fear will no longer have strongholds in your life. God will guide you over absolutely every hurdle you may ever face. He loves you, and He wants to be in your life and bless you beyond measure. Go ahead. Pick up His Word and let it bring healing and restoration to your life! Meanwhile, if you or someone you love is facing one of life's storms and is in need of an anchor, I pray that the quick reference list outlined here will be helpful. The words written in *italicized lettering* indicate anchor verses or phrases that I often meditated on throughout my cancer journey. Remember: if you can worry, then you already know how to meditate! Surrender yourself and all of your inadequacies to the one who holds you in the palm of His *victorious* right hand. *Dangle* those feet in complete freedom, understanding that He loves you and that He will never let you go!

Quick Reference: Scriptures

Faith

- Consider it pure joy, my brothers and sisters, whenever you face trials of many kinds, because you know that the testing of your faith develops perseverance. Let perseverance finish its work so that you may be mature and complete, not lacking anything (James 1:2, 3).
- *Trust the Lord with all your heart and lean not on your own understanding. In all your ways acknowledge him and He will*

make your paths straight. Do not be wise in your own eyes; fear the Lord and shun evil. This will bring health to your body and nourishment to your bones (Proverbs 3:5–7).

- I am sure of this, that He who began a good work in you will carry it on to completion to the day of Christ Jesus (Philippians 1:6 HCSB).

- I lift up over all, the (covering) shield of saving faith, upon which I can quench all the flaming missiles of the wicked one (Ephesians 6:16 AMP).

- Let us hold on to the *confession* of our hope without wavering, for He who promised is faithful (Hebrews 10:23 HCSB).

- For it is by grace you have been saved through *faith* and this not from yourselves. It is a gift of God, not by works so that no one can boast (Ephesians 2:8–9).

- Having believed you were marked with a seal the promised Holy Spirit who is the deposit guaranteeing our inheritance until the redemption of those who are God's possession to the praise of His glory (Ephesians 1:14).

- Let us fix our eyes on Jesus, the Author and Perfecter of our faith who for the joy set before him endured the cross, scorning its shame and sat down at the right hand of the throne of God. Do not grow weary and lose heart! (Hebrews 12:2).

- Faith is being sure of what we hope for and certain of what we do not see … By faith I understand that the universe was formed at God's command, so that what is seen was not made out of what was visible (Hebrews 11:1, 3).

- Without faith it is impossible to please and be satisfactory to Him. For whoever would come near to God must believe that God exists and that He is the rewarder of those who earnestly and diligently seek Him [out] (Hebrews 11:6 AMP).
- I assure you: If anyone says to this mountain, Be lifted up and thrown into the sea, and does not doubt in his heart, but believes that what he says will happen, it will be done for him (Mark 11:23 HCSB).
- For we hold that a man is justified and made upright by faith independent of and distinctly apart from good deeds (works of the law) (Romans 3:28 AMP).
- May the God of your hope so fill you with all joy and peace in believing [through the experience of your faith] that by the power of the Holy Spirit you may abound and be overflowing (bubbling over) with hope (Romans 15:13 AMP).
- *For we walk by faith, not by sight (2 Corinthians 5:7 ESV).*
- Because of our faith in Him, we dare to have the boldness (courage and confidence) of free access to God with freedom and without fear (Ephesians 3:12 AMP).

Rest, Peace, and True Trust

- I will lie down and rest in peace, for you alone O Lord, make me to dwell in safety (Psalm 4:8).
- *See, I am sending an angel ahead of you to guard you along the way and to bring you to the place I have prepared (Exodus 23:20).*
- The Name of the Lord is a strong tower; The righteous man runs into it and is safe! (Proverbs 18:10 ESV).

- Therefore I tell you, do not worry about your life (Matthew 6:25).
- Peace I leave with you; my peace I give you. I do not give to you as the world gives. Do not let your hearts be troubled and do not be afraid (John 14:27).
- Can any of you by worrying add a single hour to his life? (Matthew 6:27).
- *Do not be anxious about anything, but in everything, by prayer and petition, with thanksgiving, present your requests to God And the peace of God that transcends all understanding will guard your heart and mind in Christ Jesus (Philippians 4:6–7).*
- Come to me, all ye who are weary, and burdened, and I will give you rest (Matthew 11:28).
- Therefore do not worry about tomorrow, for tomorrow will worry about itself (Matthew 6:34).

Healing

- *Your light shall break forth like the morning, and your healing (my restoration and the power of a new life) shall spring forth speedily; then your righteousness will go before you and the glory of the Lord will guard you from behind (Isaiah 58:8 AMP).*
- The Lord has declared that He will restore me to health and heal my wounds (Jeremiah 30:17 AMP).
- Heal me, O Lord, and I shall be healed; save me, and I shall be saved, for You are my praise (Jeremiah 17:14 AMP).
- Let all that I am praise the Lord; may I never forget the good things he does for me. He forgives all my sins and heals all my diseases (Psalm 103:2–3 NLT).

- Is anyone among you sick? Let them call the elders of the church to pray over them and anoint them with oil in the name of the Lord. And the prayer *offered in faith will make the sick person well;* the Lord will raise them up (James 5:14–15).

- He sent His word and *healed* them; He *rescued* them from the pit (Psalm 107:20 HCSB).

- I will not die, but I will live and proclaim what the LORD has done (Psalm 118:17 HCSB).

- *He heals the brokenhearted and binds up their wounds* (curing their pains and their sorrows) (Psalm 147:3 AMP).

- He Himself bore our sins in His body on the cross, so that we might die to sin and live to righteousness; *For by His wounds you were healed* (1 Peter 2:24 NAS).

Help

- The Lord is my Strength and my impenetrable Shield; my heart trusts in, relies on, and confidently leans on Him, and I am helped; therefore my heart greatly rejoices and with my song will I praise Him (Psalm 28:7 AMP).

- And call on Me in the day of trouble; I will deliver you, and you shall honor and glorify Me (Psalm 50:15 AMP).

- *Cast your burdens on the LORD, and He will sustain you; He will never allow the righteous to be shaken* (Psalm 55:22 HCSB).

- Unless the LORD had given me help, I would soon have dwelt in the silence of death. When I said, "My foot is slipping," Your unfailing love, LORD, supported me. When anxiety was great within me, your consolation brought me joy (Psalm 94:17–19 HCSB).

- Teach me to do your will for you are my God May Your gracious Spirit lead me on level ground. Because of Your name, Yahweh, let me live in Your righteousness, deliver me from trouble (Psalm 143:10–11 HCSB).

- For I the Lord God hold your right hand; I am the Lord, Who says to me, Fear not; I will help you! (Isaiah 41:13 AMP).

- The Lord is good, a *strength and stronghold* in my day of trouble; He knows those who take refuge and trust in Him (Nahum 1:7 AMP).

- He gives strength to the weary and strengthens the powerless (Isaiah 40:29 HCSB).

- You, LORD, will keep the needy safe and will protect us forever from the wicked (Psalm 12:7).

- So we take comfort and are encouraged and confidently and boldly say, The Lord is my Helper; I will not be seized with alarm (I will not fear or dread or be terrified). What can man do to me? (Hebrews 13:6 AMP).

- Taste and see that the LORD is good, blessed is the one who takes refuge in Him (Psalm 34:8).

Fear

- The LORD is my Light and Salvation, whom shall I fear or dread? The Lord is the Refuge and Stronghold of my life, of whom shall I be afraid? (Psalm 27:1).

- God will cover me with his wings; I will be *safe* in his care; his faithfulness will *protect* and *defend* me. I need not fear any dangers at night or sudden attacks during the day (Psalm 91:4–5).

- They will have no fear of receiving bad news; their hearts are steadfast, trusting in the LORD. Their hearts are secure, they have no fear; in the end they will look in triumph on their foes (Psalm 112: 7, 8).
- Fear of a man will prove to be a snare, but whoever trusts in the LORD, is kept safe (Proverbs 29:25).
- Do not be seized with alarm and struck with fear, little flock, for it is your Father's good pleasure to give you the kingdom (Luke 12:32 AMP).
- For God has not given us the spirit of fear and timidity, but of power, love, and self-discipline (2 Timothy 1:7 NLT).
- Have I not commanded you? Be strong and courageous. Do not be afraid; do not be discouraged, for the LORD your God will be with you wherever you go (Joshua 1:9).
- There is no fear in love (dread does not exist) but full-grown (complete, perfect) love turns fear out of doors and expels every trace of terror! (1 John 4:18 AMP).

Victory

- *Don't be afraid, for I am with you. Don't be discouraged, for I am your God. I will strengthen you and help you. I will hold you up with my VICTORIOUS right hand!* (Isaiah 41:10 NLT).
- You dear children, are from God and have overcome them because the One who is in you is greater than the one who is in the world (1 John 4:4).

- *For I know the plans I have for you, declares the LORD, plans to prosper you and not to harm you. Plans to give you a hope and a future. Then you will call upon me and come and pray to me and I will listen to you. You will seek me and find me when you seek me with all your heart. I will be found by you declares the LORD and bring you back from captivity* (Jeremiah 29:11–14).

- When this perishable puts on the imperishable and this that was capable of dying puts on freedom from death, then shall be fulfilled the Scripture that says, Death is swallowed up (vanquished forever) in and unto victory. Thanks be to God, Who gives us the victory (making us conquerors) through the Lord Jesus Christ (1 Corinthians 15:54, 57 AMP).

- Because the Lord God helps me, I will not be dismayed; therefore, I have set my face like flint to do his will and I know that I will *triumph* (Isaiah 50:7).

- Amid all these things, I am more than a conqueror and gain a surpassing victory through Him who loves me (Romans 8:37).

- For every child of God defeats this evil world by trusting Christ to give the victory. The ones who win this battle against the world are the ones who believe that Jesus is the Son of God (1 John 5:3–5).

Appendix B

Help for the Body

As I mentioned earlier, the battle against cancer does not stop with the end of formal treatment. While I did not search the Internet for information about the type of cancer with which I was diagnosed, I researched general causes of cancer and the nutritional deficits that may make a person vulnerable to cancer. I wanted to know the *facts*, which can be like searching for a needle in a haystack with all of the *opinions* that can easily be found on the Internet. Some people advocate one diet over another. Some say go all-out organic, while others believe only certain foods need to be organic. Some say no artificial sweeteners, while others say no sugar. It's all confusing to say the least!

Here I have included some simple ways I have adapted my daily diet to incorporate what I have learned. I by no means have all the answers. In fact, I probably still have more questions than answers. Whether or not your life has included a cancer diagnosis until this point, I believe this list represents a good, general guideline to follow for optimal health. When a person has cancer, it often indicates the person has multiple nutritional deficiencies. These could be due to genetic, environmental, nutritional, and lifestyle factors. To overcome multiple nutritional deficiencies, changing one's diet can improve overall health and strengthen the immune system. When a person's immune system is strong enough, cancer cells can be destroyed and prevented from multiplying and forming tumors in the body. Who doesn't want that? There is no one diet, one food, one strategy, or one treatment that will guarantee a life free from cancer. For survivors, the quest to win over cancer continues long after the medical treatment ends. We can't control whether a reoccurrence happens, but we sure can live each day knowing we're giving our bodies the nutrients it needs—and the best chance of survival—by maintaining a healthy diet with a few simple truths in mind. Following are the basic guidelines I have chosen to follow the past few years:

Quick Reference: Nutrition

1. I focus on a plant-based diet that includes a variety of nonstarchy vegetables, fruits, nuts, whole grains, seeds, and legumes. I eat them in their natural state whenever possible, minimizing processing, cooking, peeling, and mixing with other ingredients. Cooked food represents only about 25 percent of my daily diet.

2. I usually kick my day off with a smoothie consisting of baby spinach, fresh or frozen organic fruit, Greek yogurt, and chia seeds with either almond milk or coconut water. This boosts my energy and my metabolism and gets me off to a great start!

3. I buy organic or local produce when possible. I wash these foods thoroughly with a natural fruit and veggie cleaner. I keep a copy of my two lists, "Clean Fifteen" and the "Dirty Dozen," in my purse to remind me which fruits and veggies are worth the extra money to buy organic. See these lists in the upcoming pages.

4. I exercise at least thirty minutes four to five times a week. I simply feel better when I'm active, and the AICR is adamant that keeping your body mass index low is vital to cancer prevention. Exercising gives me energy and keeps my joint pain to a minimum.

5. I avoid processed foods whenever possible. If you check labels, you will find that processed foods typically contain more sugar and/or sodium than unprocessed foods. I believe the more you consume whole foods in their original state, the better. Eat an apple instead of drinking apple juice. Eat a sweet potato instead of candied yams. Eat grapes instead of raisins, and so on.

6. I minimize my consumption of animal-based products. If I eat animal sources of protein, I look for meat from animals that had happy lives, such as grass-fed beef, cage-free poultry, wild-caught salmon, and so on.

7. I try to get 25 to 30 grams of fiber a day. Fiber helps keep food moving through your digestive tract and moves cancer-causing compounds out before they can create harm. I focus on fruits, vegetables, and whole grains that are high in fiber. There is no fiber in meat, dairy, sugar, or white foods like processed white bread, white rice, pastries, and so on.

8. It has been my experience that cancer is a disease that affects the body, mind, and spirit. I work diligently to keep a proactive outlook and positive attitude. I believe that anger, unforgiveness, fear, bitterness, and stress raise your cortisol level, which in turn may compromise your body in its fight to prevent cancer. I recommend we all learn to have a loving and forgiving spirit and choose to relax, be content, and enjoy life. My soul is often renewed by praying, meditating on God's Word, listening to uplifting music, and spending time with those who love, support, and encourage me.

9. I minimize the amount of saturated fats and trans fats in my diet, only rarely eating red meat, dairy products, or eggs. I know there is much controversy over the benefits of eggs, and I love a good egg, so I just wait and eat them when I'm really craving them. I stick with fat sources like olive oil, canola oil, nuts, and avocados. Coconut oil has become quite the craze lately, and I do use it from time to time; however, I still think minimizing the amount of saturated fats you allow into your diet is wise.

10. I *love* berries! I eat blackberries, blueberries, or strawberries practically every day. I only eat strawberries if they are organic since they are on the Dirty Dozen list. I will either use berries in my smoothies, include them as a dessert, or eat them as a snack.

11. I have increased my intake of omega-3 fatty acids. I have done this by increasing my daily fish oil supplement as well as by incorporating salmon, tuna, flaxseed, and raw nuts into my diet.

12. I minimize the amount of sugar in my diet. I also prefer not to use artificial sweeteners, though sometimes I have to. I prefer natural sweeteners like local honey, Stevia, and monk fruit. I keep packs or a small bottle of monk fruit in my purse to avoid being out and stuck without a natural sweetener.

13. I love dark chocolate! I like taking a small block of 75 to 85 percent cacao and mixing it with a small amount of sweetened coconut as a treat. I no longer indulge myself with my favorite desserts that are high in sugar. Instead I know I'm using food to help me fight cancer rather than allowing food to have a hold on my weight. This provides me with a great sense of accomplishment and contentment! I sometime use fruit as my dessert as well.

Disclaimer: This information is intended for educational purposes only and is not a substitute for advice, diagnosis, or treatment by a licensed physician. You should seek prompt medical care for any health issues and consult your doctor before taking dietary supplements or making any major dietary changes.

Recommendations for Cancer Prevention from the American Institute for Cancer Research

These ten recommendations for cancer prevention are drawn from the WCRF/AICR Second Expert Report.

1. Be as lean as possible without becoming underweight.
2. Be physically active for at least thirty minutes every day. Limit sedentary habits.
3. Avoid sugary drinks. Limit consumption of energy-dense foods.
4. Eat more of a variety of vegetables, fruit, whole grains, lentils, and beans.
5. Limit consumption of red meats (such as beef, pork, and lamb) and avoid processed meats (deli meats, sausages, hot dogs).
6. If consumed at all, limit alcoholic beverages to two for men and one for women a day.
7. Limit consumption of salty foods and foods processed with salt (sodium).
8. Don't depend solely on supplements to protect against cancer.
9. It is best for mothers to breastfeed exclusively for up to six months and then add other liquids and foods.
10. After treatment cancer survivors should follow the recommendations for cancer prevention.

The Dirty Dozen

According to EWG's 2015 Shopper's Guide to Pesticides in Produce

(Buy organic if possible.)

1. Apples

2. Strawberries

3. Grapes

4. Celery

5. Peaches

6. Spinach

7. Sweet bell peppers

8. Nectarines (imported)

9. Cucumbers

10. Cherry tomatoes

11. Snap peas (imported)

12. Potatoes

The Clean Fifteen

According to EWG's 2015 Shopper's Guide to Pesticides in Produce

(There's no need to buy organic for these.)

1. Avocados

2. Sweet corn

3. Pineapples

4. Cabbage

5. Sweet peas (frozen)

6. Onions

7. Asparagus

8. Mangoes

9. Papayas

10. Kiwi

11. Eggplant

12. Grapefruit

13. Cantaloupe

14. Cauliflower

15. Sweet potatoes

Appendix C

Lyrics to "Trust" by David Stewart

Trust (Proverbs 3:5–6)   Key:B, 4/4, 70 bpm
Arranged and adapted by David Stewart

Verse
(First verse and chorus sung by soloist)
Trust in the Lord with all your heart
Lean not on your understanding
Trust in the Lord with all your heart
Lean not on your understanding

Chorus
In all your ways acknowledge Him
And He will direct your paths
Trust in the Lord with all your heart
Trust in the Lord
Trust in the Lord

Verse
(Ladies join soloist)
Trust in the Lord with all your heart
Lean not on your understanding

Trust in the Lord with all your heart
Lean not on your understanding

Chorus
In all your ways acknowledge Him
And He will direct your paths
Trust in the Lord with all your heart
Trust in the Lord
Trust in the Lord

Bridge

(Full Choir)	*(Lyrics created and sung by soloist -Amy Carr)*
Trust Trust (Repeat 2x)	When the dark clouds come Lord, I will not, I will not walk in fear, oh no I won't.
Trust Trust (Repeat 2x)	When the waves of doubt overwhelm me Lord, in You I will trust. In the midst of my struggle Lord, I know, you'll never, never
Trust Trust	leave me. Resting in your right hand Lord, that's where I want to be. I know by your stripes Lord, I've already been healed, oh yes I have!
Trust Trust	So all of my faith Lord, all of my hope, and all of my TRUST is in You

Verse
(Full choir, Soloist's adlibs vary and continue to end of song)
Trust in the Lord with all your heart
Lean not on your understanding
Trust in the Lord with all your heart
Lean not on your understanding

Chorus
In all your ways acknowledge Him
And He will direct your paths
Trust in the Lord with all your heart

Tag

Trust in the Lord
Trust in the Lord
Trust in the Lord

For Trust and other original praise and worship music by David Stewart, please visit www.chworship.com.

Author Biography

Amy grew up in Strawberry Plains, TN with her parents and older brother. As a child, she was somewhat of a "tomboy" who loved playing basketball and softball. She accepted Jesus as her Savior at the age of eight. Amy enjoys the benefits of having a large extended family who share the values of faith in God, family, and enjoying life. She met her husband, David, at Calvary Baptist Church in Knoxville, TN in January 1989. They were later married there in July 1991. God blessed them with the privilege of finalizing their adoption of both of their children, Kayla and Anthony, in December 1998. Amy enjoys boating on the lakes of east Tennessee, cooking out, movie nights, singing in the choir, "Thursday night dinners" at her parents' house, spontaneous getaways with her husband, and family beach vacations. Amy earned her Bachelor of Arts degree from the University of Tennessee in Knoxville. She has worked as a social worker serving youth and their families in the East Tennessee area for twenty eight years. The last twenty years of her career were spent working at Omni Visions, a multi-state placement agency for children and adults. Amy worked in the children's division as a Resource Coordinator providing therapeutic foster care and adoption services for children in state's custody. She was diagnosed with bilateral breast cancer in April 2011 and completed her treatment in September 2012. In May 2015, she was diagnosed with Acute Promyelocytic Leukemia (aka: APL or M3) and is currently undergoing treatment. Thankfully, her prognosis is once again very good. Since retiring from Omni Visions in June 2014, Amy has focused on caring for her family, finalizing and publishing *Dangling,* and speaking to various women's groups, bible study groups, and churches. Many have found Amy's transparency, humor, and down to earth style of speaking both encouraging and refreshing. Her determination to walk by faith in God and His promises through life's challenges is evident to all who know her. Her uplifting spirit and resolve to fight a good fight of faith from the position of victory, peace and rest inspires others to want to do the same.

For information about booking a speaking engagement with Amy for your bible study group, women's group, church, or breast cancer awareness event, contact her at amy@amycarrbooks.com.

Made in the USA
Coppell, TX
30 March 2022

75760108R00092